The Promises Guidebook

A Handbook For Appropriating Divine Promises In Your Life

by Allan and Kathy Kiuna

The Promises Guidebook
A Handbook for Appropriating Divine Promises In Your Life

Copyright © 2010 Allan & Kathy Kiuna
Jubilee Christian Church
P. O. Box 33790 - 00600
Nairobi, Kenya

Telephone (+254) 719 777 222

Email: bishop@jcckenya.net
Web site: www.jcckenya.net

Unless otherwise stated, scripture quotations
are taken from the
King James Version of the Bible
All rights reserved.

No part of this book may be reproduced or transmitted
in any form or by any means, electronic or mechanical,
including photocopy, recording
or any information storage and retrieval systems,
except as provided by the copyright law.

Published in Kenya in 2010 by Jubilee Publishers

Table of Contents

Preface 6

PART 1 - FOUNDATIONS OF GOD'S PROMISES
1. What is a promise? 8
2. Why are promises important? 8
3. How do we obtain the promises? 8
4. God's Commitment to His Promises 11

PART 2 - THE BIBLE IS YOUR ...
5. Infallible authority 13
6. Deed of Inheritance 15
7. The guide of life 18
8. Stability 21
9. Strength 23

PART 3: WHAT THE BIBLE PROMISES ABOUT ...
10. Authority of the believer 26
11. The desires of your heart 27
12. Faith in God 28
13. New life 31
14. Failure and helplessness 32
15. Forgiveness 33
16. God's faithfulness 35
17. Giving and Charity 40
18. Decision making 42
19. Heaven 43
20. The second coming of Christ 44
21. Justification 46
22. Prayer 47
23. The power for God's service 49
24. Spiritual growth 50
25. God's Wisdom 51
26. God's grace and favour 53

27. The truth of God's Word..56
28. Trusting God..57

PART 4: WHAT TO DO WHEN YOU FEEL...

29. Anxious..60
30. Condemned..61
31. Confused..62
32. Depressed..63
33. Hopeless..64
34. Lonely..66

PART 5: WHAT TO DO WHEN YOU ARE...

35. Experiencing sufferings, difficulties and attacks from people... 69
36. ...and demonic attacks..72
37. Having marital problems..75
38. In Financial Crisis..78
39. In times of fear and doubt..82
40. Waiting on God..85

PART 6: WHAT TO DO WHEN YOU NEED...

41. Comfort..88
42. Courage..90
43. Inspiration..92
44. Joy..93
45. Strength..99

PART 7: GOD'S PROMISE CONCERNING...

46. Abundance..102
47. Eternal life..103
48. Eternal honour..104
49. Family..105
50. Freedom..108

51. Guidance 110
52. Health and healing 113
53. His presence 115
54. His unfailing Love 116
55. His Word 118
56. Holy Spirit 120
57. Justice 122
58. Knowledge 123
59. Long life 124
60. Marriage 125
61. Peace 127
62. Practical physical needs 130
63. Promotion 133
64. Prosperity 134
65. Protection 143
66. His Love 145
67. Rest 147
68. Restoration 148
69. Salvation 149
70. Spiritual gifts 151
71. Success 152
72. Widows 153
73. Mercy 155

Preface

Have you ever been promised something by someone who failed to deliver? The disappointment must have been terrible! In our world, fewer and fewer people believe or accept promises. But I have great news! I know someone whose promises you and I can truly believe because He does not over-promise or under-deliver. His name is God and His promises are rock solid and totally dependable.

The bible says in Numbers 23:19:

"God is not a man, that He should lie; neither the son of man, that He should repent: Hath He said, and shall He not do it? Or hath he spoken, and shall he not make it good?"

When God promises anything, it is better and surer than a banker's cheque. God's word is full of beautiful and incredible promises that do not bounce.

Whatever God promises, HE MAKES GOOD!

Bishop Allan Kiuna

Part 1

Foundations of God's Promises

What is a promise?

A promise is a commitment to do something.

It is a declaration of an intention to act.

Moreover, a promise is a pledge or a vow that declares an intention to finish a task.

It is a solemn assurance to grant a certain specified thing.

Why are promises important?

They reveal to us the agenda of God over our lives

Promises give us the foundation of hope and faith

They reveal God's commitment to us

Promises create focus and have the power to direct us to our goals

They generate the passion for pursuit

Promises empower us and give us a right to possess.

How do we obtain God's promises?

1. You must be convinced that God cannot lie.

His promises are communicated via His word and His word has been tested.

Psa.18:30
"As for God, His way is perfect: the word of the Lord is tried: he is a buckler to all those that trust in Him"

Psa.12:6
"The words of the Lord are pure words: as silver tried in a furnace of earth, purified seven times."

Num.23:19
"God is not a man, that He should lie; neither the son of man, that He should repent: Hath He said, and shall He not do it? Or hath he spoken, and shall he not make it good?"

2. You must, against all odds, believe in hope.
The bible talks of Abraham having hoped against hope in order to obtain the promises.

Rom.4:18
"Who against hope believed in hope, that he might become the father of many nations, according to that which was spoken, So shall thy seed be."

3. Do not be weak in faith.
The bible says:

Rom.14:23
"And he that doubteth is damned if he eat, because he eateth not of faith: for whatsoever is not of faith is sin."

Heb.10:23
"Let us hold fast the profession of our faith without wavering; for he is faithful that promised."

Heb.11:6
"But without faith it is impossible to please him: for he that cometh to God must believe that he is, and that he is a rewarder of them that diligently seek him."

4. Stagger not, waver not, and get rid of the second opinion. Be focused.

James 1:6
"...for he who doubts is like a wave of the sea driven and tossed by the wind. For let not that man suppose that he will receive anything from the Lord; he is a double-minded man, unstable in all his ways."

5. Be fully persuaded

Rom.4:21
"And being fully persuaded that, what he had promised, he was able also to perform."

Rom.14:5
"One man esteemeth one day above another: another esteemeth every day alike. Let every man be fully persuaded in his own mind."

2 Corinthians 7:1
"Having therefore these promises, dearly beloved, let us cleanse ourselves from all filthiness of the flesh and spirit, perfecting holiness in the fear of God."

> **"God has given no pledge which He will not redeem, and encouraged no hope which He will not fulfil."**

Foundations of God's Promises

God's Commitment To His Promises

Num.23:19
God is not a man that He should lie, nor a son of man that He should change His mind.

Heb.10:23
Let us hold fast the confession of our hope without wavering, for He who promised is faithful.

Isa.46:11
Indeed I have spoken it; I will also bring it to pass. I have purposed it; I will also do it.

Ps 89:34
My covenant I will not break, Nor alter the word that has gone out of My lips. Once I have sworn by My holiness; I will not lie to David..."

Part 2

The Bible is Your...

The Bible Is Your ...

Infallible authority

2 Timothy 3:16
All scripture is given by inspiration of God, and is profitable for doctrine, for reproof, for correction, for instruction in righteousness:

2 Peter 1:20-21
Knowing this first, that no prophecy of the scripture is of any private interpretation. For the prophecy came not in old time by the will of man: but holy men of God spake as they were moved by the Holy Ghost.

Hebrews 4:12
For the word of God is quick, and powerful, and sharper than any two edged sword, piercing even to the dividing asunder of soul and spirit, and of the joints and marrow, and is a discerner of the thoughts and intents of the heart.

Isaiah 55:10-11
For as the rain cometh down, and the snow from heaven, and returneth not thither, but watereth the earth, and maketh it bring forth and bud, that it may give seed to the sower, and bread to the eater: So shall my word be that goeth forth out of my mouth: it shall not return unto me void, but it shall accomplish that which I please, and it shall prosper in the thing whereto I sent it.

The Promises Guidebook

John 5:39
Search the scriptures; for in them ye think ye have eternal life: and they are they which testify of me.

1 Peter 1:23
Being born again, not of corruptible seed, but of incorruptible, by the word of God, which liveth and abideth for ever.

Psalms 33:9
For He spake, and it was done; He commanded, and it stood fast.

Proverbs 30:5
Every word of God is pure: He is a shield unto them that put their trust in Him.

Psalms 119:89
For ever, O Lord, thy word is settled in heaven.

Psalms 33:6
By the word of the Lord were the heavens made; and all the host of them by the breath of his mouth.

2 Corinthians 1:20
For all the promises of God in him are yea, and in him Amen, unto the glory of God by us.

1 Peter 1:24-25
For all flesh is as grass, and all the glory of man as the flower of grass. The grass withereth, and the flower thereof falleth away: But the word of the Lord endureth for ever. And this is the word which by the gospel is preached unto you.

Mark 13:31
Heaven and earth shall pass away: but my words shall not pass away.

Deed Of Inheritance

Acts 20:32
And now, brethren, I commend you to God, and to the word of his grace, which is able to build you up, and to give you an inheritance among all them which are sanctified.

Acts 26:18
To open their eyes, and to turn them from darkness to light, and from the power of Satan unto God, that they may receive forgiveness of sins, and inheritance among them which are sanctified by faith that is in me.

Romans 8:16-17
The Spirit itself beareth witness with our spirit, that we are the children of God: And if children, then heirs; heirs of God, and joint-heirs with Christ; if

so be that we suffer with him, that we may be also glorified together.

Ephesians 1:11-14
In whom also we have obtained an inheritance, being predestinated according to the purpose of him who worketh all things after the counsel of his own will: That we should be to the praise of his glory, who first trusted in Christ. In whom ye also trusted, after that ye heard the word of truth, the gospel of your salvation: in whom also after that ye believed, ye were sealed with that holy Spirit of promise, which is the earnest of our inheritance until the redemption of the purchased possession, unto the praise of his glory.

Galatians 3:29
And if ye be Christ's, then are ye Abraham's seed, and heirs according to the promise.

Ephesians 3:6
That the Gentiles should be fellowheirs, and of the same body, and partakers of his promise in Christ by the gospel:

John 14:2-3
In my Father's house are many mansions: if it were not so, I would have told you. I go to prepare a place for you. And if I go and prepare a place for you, I will come again, and receive you unto myself; that where I am, there ye may be also.

The Bible Is Your ...

Hebrews 11:16
But now they desire a better country, that is, an heavenly: wherefore God is not ashamed to be called their God: for he hath prepared for them a city.

Matthew 25:34
Then shall the King say unto them on his right hand, Come, ye blessed of my Father, inherit the kingdom prepared for you from the foundation of the world:

2 Corinthians 1:20
For all the promises of God in him are yea, and in him Amen, unto the glory of God by us.

1 Peter 1:3-4
Blessed be the God and Father of our Lord Jesus Christ, which according to his abundant mercy hath begotten us again unto a lively hope by the resurrection of Jesus Christ from the dead, To an inheritance incorruptible, and undefiled, and that fadeth not away, reserved in heaven for you;

1 Corinthians 2:9
But as it is written, Eye hath not seen, nor ear heard, neither have entered into the heart of man, the things which God hath prepared for them that love him.

2 Peter 1:4
Whereby are given unto us exceeding great and precious promises: that by these ye might be partakers of the divine nature, having escaped the corruption that is in the world through lust.

Colossians 3:23-24
And whatever you do, do it heartily, as to the Lord and not to men, knowing that from the Lord you will receive the reward of the inheritance; for you serve the Lord Christ.

Psalms 37:34
Wait on the Lord, and keep his way, and he shall exalt thee to inherit the land: when the wicked are cut off, thou shalt see it. Lord ye shall receive the reward of the inheritance: for ye serve the Lord Christ.

The Guide Of Life

Psalms 119:105
Thy word is a lamp unto my feet, and a light unto my path.

Proverbs 6:22-23
When thou goest, it shall lead thee; when thou sleepest, it shall keep thee; and when thou awakest, it shall talk with thee. For the commandment is a lamp; and the law is light; and reproofs of instruction are the way of life:

The Bible Is Your ...

Psalms 119:11
Thy word have I hid in mine heart, that I might not sin against thee.

Psalms 19:11
Moreover by them is thy servant warned: and in keeping of them there is great reward.

Psalms 119:9
Wherewithal shall a young man cleanse his way? by taking heed thereto according to thy word.

John 8:31-32
Then said Jesus to those Jews which believed on him, If ye continue in my word, then are ye my disciples indeed; And ye shall know the truth, and the truth shall make you free.

Psalms 119:24
Thy testimonies also are my delight and my counsellors.

2 Peter 1:4
Whereby are given unto us exceeding great and precious promises: that by these ye might be partakers of the divine nature, having escaped the corruption that is in the world through lust.

Psalms 37:23
The steps of a good man are ordered by the Lord: and he delighteth in his way.

Psalms 32:8
I will instruct thee and teach thee in the way which thou shalt go: I will guide thee with mine eye.

Psalms 23:3
He restoreth my soul: he leadeth me in the paths of righteousness for his name's sake.

Isaiah 30:21
And thine ears shall hear a word behind thee, saying, This is the way, walk ye in it, when ye turn to the right hand, and when ye turn to the left.

Luke 1:79
As he spake by the mouth of his holy prophets, which have been since the world began:

Luke 1:70
To give light to them that sit in darkness and in the shadow of death, to guide our feet into the way of peace.

Joshua 1:8
This book of the law shall not depart out of thy mouth; but thou shalt meditate therein day and night, that thou mayest observe to do according to all that is written therein: for then thou shalt make thy way prosperous, and then thou shalt have good success.

The Bible Is Your ...

2 Timothy 3:16-17
All scripture is given by inspiration of God, and is profitable for doctrine, for reproof, for correction, for instruction in righteousness: That the man of God may be perfect, thoroughly furnished unto all good works.

Stability

1 Peter 1:23-25
Being born again, not of corruptible seed, but of incorruptible, by the word of God, which liveth and abideth for ever. For all flesh is as grass, and all the glory of man as the flower of grass. The grass withereth, and the flower thereof falleth away: But the word of the Lord endureth for ever. And this is the word which by the gospel is preached unto you.

Matthew 24:35
Heaven and earth shall pass away, but my words shall not pass away.

Psalms 119:89
For ever, O Lord, thy word is settled in heaven.

Isaiah 40:8
The grass withereth, the flower fadeth: but the word of our God shall stand for ever.

Matthew 5:18
For verily I say unto you, Till heaven and earth pass, one jot or one tittle shall in no wise pass from the law, till all be fulfilled.

The Promises of God

1 Kings 8:56
Blessed be the Lord, that hath given rest unto his people Israel, according to all that he promised: there hath not failed one word of all his good promise,

Ezekiel 12:25
For I am the Lord: I will speak, and the word that I shall speak shall come to pass; it shall be no more prolonged: for in your days, O rebellious house, will I say the word, and will perform it, saith the Lord GOD.

Proverbs 4:20-22
My son, attend to my words; incline thine ear unto my sayings. Let them not depart from thine eyes; keep them in the midst of thine heart. For they are life unto those that find them, and health to all their flesh.

Romans 8:21
Because the creature itself also shall be delivered from the bondage of corruption into the glorious liberty of the children of God.

The Bible Is Your ...

Strength

Daniel 10:19
And said, O man greatly beloved, fear not: peace be unto thee, be strong, yea, be strong. And when he had spoken unto me, I was strengthened, and said, Let my lord speak; for thou hast strengthened me.

Psalms 119:28
My soul melteth for heaviness: strengthen thou me according unto thy word.

Colossians 1:10-12
That ye might walk worthy of the Lord unto all pleasing, being fruitful in every good work, and increasing in the knowledge of God; Strengthened with all might, according to his glorious power, unto all patience and longsuffering with joyfulness; Giving thanks unto the Father, which hath made us meet to be partakers of the inheritance of the saints in light:

Nehemiah. 8:10
Then he said unto them, Go your way, eat the fat, and drink the sweet, and send portions unto them for whom nothing is prepared: for this day is holy unto our Lord: neither be ye sorry; for the

Proverbs 8:14
Counsel is mine, and sound wisdom: I am understanding; I have strength. joy of the Lord is your strength.

The Promises of God

Isaiah 40:29
He giveth power to the faint; and to them that have no might he increaseth strength.

Psalms 18:2
The Lord is my rock, and my fortress, and my deliverer; my God, my strength, in whom I will trust; my buckler, and the horn of my salvation, and my high tower.

Ephesians 6:13
Wherefore take unto you the whole armour of God, that ye may be able to withstand in the evil day, and having done all, to stand.

Psalms 27:1
The Lord is my light and my salvation; whom shall I fear? the Lord is the strength of my life; of whom shall I be afraid?

Ephesians 6:10
Finally, my brethren, be strong in the Lord, and in the power of his might.

Part 3

What The Bible Promises About...

Authority of the believer

Genesis 1:27-28
So God created man in his own image, in the image of God created he him; male and female created he them. And God blessed them, and God said unto them, Be fruitful, and multiply, and replenish the earth, and subdue it: and have dominion over the fish of the sea, and over the fowl of the air, and over every living thing that moveth upon the earth.

Genesis 9:2
And the fear of you and the dread of you shall be upon every beast of the earth, and upon every fowl of the air, upon all that moveth upon the earth, and upon all the fishes of the sea; into your hand are they delivered.

2 Samuel 22:30
For by thee I have run through a troop: by my God have I leaped over a wall.

Luke 10:19
Behold, I give unto you power to tread on serpents and scorpions, and over all the power of the enemy: and nothing shall by any means hurt you.

Ephesians 1:19
And what is the exceeding greatness of his power to us-ward who believe, according to the working of his mighty power,

Ephesians 1:22-23
And hath put all things under his feet, and gave him to be the head over all things to the church, Which is his body, the fulness of him that filleth all in all.

The desires of your heart

Ps.20:4
May He give you the desire of your heart and make all your plans succeed.

Ps.21:2
You have given him his heart's desire, and have not withheld the request of his lips.

Prov.10:24
The fear of the wicked will come upon him, and the desire of the righteous will be granted.

Ps.103:4-5
Who redeems your life from destruction, Who crowns you with loving kindness and tender mercies, Who satisfies your mouth with good things, So that your youth is renewed like theeagle's.

Mark 11:24
Therefore I say to you, whatever things you ask when you pray, believe that you receive them, and you will have them.

The Promises of God

Faith in God

Rom.12:3

Think of yourself... in accordance with the measure of faith God has given you.

Eph.2:8
For by grace you have been saved through faith, and that not of yourselves; it is the gift of God, not of works, lest anyone should boast.

Heb.11:6
But without faith it is impossible to please Him, for he who comes to God must believe that He is and that He is a rewarder of those who diligently seek Him.

James 1:3
Knowing that the testing of your faith produces patience.

1 Peter 1:7
That the genuineness of your faith, being much more precious than gold that perishes, though it is tested by fire, may be found to praise, honour, and glory at the revelation of Jesus Christ.

Rom 1:17
For in it the righteousness of God is revealed from faith to faith; as it is written, "The just shall live by faith."

What The Bible Promises About...

1 John 5:4
For whatever is born of God overcomes the world. And this is the victory that has overcome the world — our faith.

Mark 9:23
Jesus said to him, "If you can believe, all things are possible to him who believes."

Eph.6:16
Above all, taking the shield of faith with which you will be able to quench all the fiery darts of the wicked one.

John 20:29
Jesus said to him, "Thomas, because you have seen Me, you have believed. Blessed are those who have not seen and yet have believed."

Matt.21:21-22
So Jesus answered and said to them, "Assuredly, I say to you, if you have faith and do not doubt, you will not only do what was done to the fig tree, but also if you say to this mountain, 'Be removed and be cast into the sea,' it will be done. And whatever things you ask in prayer, believing, you will receive."

John 16:24
Until now you have asked nothing in My name. Ask, and you will receive, that your joy may be full.

John 12:46
"I have come into the world as light, so that no one who believes in me should stay in darkness."

John 1:12
" Yet to all who received him, to those who believed in his name, he gave the right to become children of God."

Heb.11:1
"Now faith is being sure of what we hope for and certain of what we do not see.

Gal. 3:26
"You are all sons of God through faith in Christ Jesus"

2 Cor. 5:7
For we walk by faith, not by sight.

What The Bible Promises About...

New life

<u>2 Cor.5:17</u>
Therefore, if anyone is in Christ he is a new creation, the old has gone the new has come!

<u>John 10:10 NKJV</u>
The thief does not come except to steal, and to kill, and to destroy. I have come that they may have life, and that they may have it more abundantly.

<u>1 Peter 2:24 NKJV</u>
*who Himself bore our sins in His own body on the tree, that we, having died to sins, might live f
or righteousness — by whose stripes you were healed*

<u>Gal.2:20</u>
*I have been crucified with Christ; it is no longer I who live, but Christ lives in me; and the life which I now live in the flesh I live by faith in the Son of God, who loved me and gave Himself
for me.*

<u>Rom.6:4 NKJV</u>
Therefore we were buried with Him through baptism into death, that just as Christ was raised from the dead by the glory of the Father, even so we also should walk in newness of life.

1 John 3:9
Whoever has been born of God does not sin, for His seed remains in him; and he cannot sin, because he has been born of God.

2 Cor 3:18 NKJV
But we all, with unveiled face, beholding as in a mirror the glory of the Lord, are being transformed into the same image from glory to glory, just as by the Spirit of the Lord.

Ezek.36:26
I will give you a new heart and put a new spirit within you; I will take the heart of stone out of y our flesh and give you a heart of flesh.

Failure and helplessness

John 14:1
Do not let your hearts be troubled. Trust in God; Trust also in Me.

Ps.147:3
He heals the brokenhearted and binds up their wounds.

Rom.8:28
And we know that all things work together for good to those who love God, to those who are the called according to His purpose.

Isa.41:13
For I, the Lord your God, will hold your right hand, Saying to you, 'Fear not, I will help you.'

2 Cor.12:9
And He said to me, "My grace is sufficient for you, for My strength is made perfect in weakness. "Therefore most gladly I will rather boast in my infirmities, that the power of Christ may rest up on me.

Rom.8:26
Likewise the Spirit also helps in our weaknesses. For we do not know what we should pray for as we ought, but the Spirit Himself makes intercession for us with groanings which cannot be uttered.

Heb.13:6
So we may boldly say: "The Lord is my helper; I will not fear. What can man do to me?"

1 John 4:4
You are of God, little children, and have overcome them, because He who is in you is greater than he who is in the world.

Forgiveness

1 John 1:9
If we confess our sins, He is Faithful and Just and will forgive us our sins and purify us from all unrighteousness.

Ps.32:1-2
Blessed is he whose transgression is forgiven, whose sin is covered. Blessed is the man to whom the Lord does not impute iniquity, And in whose spirit there is no deceit.

Isa.43:25
"I, even I, am He who blots out your transgressions for My own sake; And I will not remember your sins.

2 Chron 7:14
If My people who are called by My name will humble themselves, and pray and seek My face, and turn from their wicked ways, then I will hear from heaven, and will forgive their sin and heal their land.

Eph 1:7
In Him we have redemption through His blood, the forgiveness of sins, according to the riches of His grace.

Matt 6:14
"For if you forgive men their trespasses, your heavenly Father will also forgive you.

Ps.103:12
As far as the east is from the west, So far has He removed our transgressions from us.

1 John 2:12
I write to you, little children, Because your sins are forgiven you for His name's sake.

Eph.1:7
"Know therefore that the Lord your God is God; he is the faithful God, keeping his covenant of love to a thousand generations of those who love him and keep his commands."

Rom.8:33
Who shall bring a charge against God's elect? It is God who justifies.

God's faithfulness

Deut.7:9
"Know therefore that the Lord your God is God; he is the faithful God, keeping his covenant of love to a thousand generations of those who love him and keep his commands."

Psalms 119:65
Thou hast dealt well with thy servant, O Lord, according unto thy word.

Thessalonians 5:24
Faithful is he that calleth you, who also will do it.

Isaiah 54:9-10
For this is as the waters of Noah unto me: for as I have sworn that the waters of Noah should no more go over the earth; so have I sworn that I would not be wroth with thee, nor rebuke thee. For the mountains shall depart, and the hills be removed; but my kindness shall not depart from thee, neither

shall the covenant of my peace be removed, saith the Lord that hath mercy on thee.

Psalms 145:18-19
The Lord is nigh unto all them that call upon him, to all that call upon him in truth. He will fulfil the desire of them that fear him: he also will hear their cry, and will save them.

Genesis 28:15
And, behold, I am with thee, and will keep thee in all places whither thou goest, and will bring thee again into this land; for I will not leave thee, until I have done that which I have spoken to thee of.

Joshua 23:14
And, behold, this day I am going the way of all the earth: and ye know in all your hearts and in all your souls, that not one thing hath failed of all the good things which the Lord your God spake concerning you; all are come to pass unto you, and not one thing hath failed thereof.

1 Kings 8:56
Blessed be the Lord, that hath given rest unto his people Israel, according to all that he promised: there hath not failed one word of all his good promise, which he promised by the hand of Moses his servant.

Psalms 36:5
Thy mercy, O Lord, is in the heavens; and thy faithfulness reacheth unto the clouds.

What The Bible Promises About...

Psalms 89:1-2
I will sing of the mercies of the Lord for ever: with my mouth will I make known thy faithfulness to all generations. For I have said, Mercy shall be built up for ever: thy faithfulness shalt thou establish in the very heavens.

Psalms 89:33-34
Nevertheless my loving kindness will I not utterly take from him, nor suffer my faithfulness to fail. My covenant will I not break, nor alter the thing that is gone out of my lips.

1 Corinthians 1:9
God is faithful, by whom ye were called unto the fellowship of his Son Jesus Christ our Lord.

1 Corinthians 10:13
There hath no temptation taken you but such as is common to man: but God is faithful, who will not suffer you to be tempted above that ye are able; but will with the temptation also make a way to escape, that ye may be able to bear it.

2 Peter 3:9
The Lord is not slack concerning his promise, as some men count slackness; but is longsuffering to usward, not willing that any should perish, but that all should come to repentance.

2 Timothy 2:13
If we believe not, yet he abideth faithful: he cannot deny himself.

Hebrews 11:11
Through faith also Sara herself received strength to conceive seed, and was delivered of a child when she was past age, because she judged him faithful who had promised.

1 Peter 4:19
Wherefore let them that suffer according to the will of God commit the keeping of their souls to him in well doing, as unto a faithful Creator.

1 John 1:9
If we confess our sins, he is faithful and just to forgive us our sins, and to cleanse us from all unrighteousness.

Jeremiah 42:5
Then they said to Jeremiah, The Lord be a true and faithful witness between us, if we do not even according to all things for the which the Lord thy God shall send thee to us.

Isaiah 49:7
Thus saith the Lord, the Redeemer of Israel, and his Holy One, to him whom man despiseth, to him whom the nation abhorreth, to a servant of rulers, Kings shall see and arise, princes also shall worship, because of the Lord that is faithful, and the Holy One of Israel, and he shall choose thee.

Psalms 119:138
Thy testimonies that thou hast commanded are righteous and very faithful.

What The Bible Promises About...

Revelation 1:5
And from Jesus Christ, who is the faithful witness, and the first begotten of the dead, and the prince of the kings of the earth. Unto him that loved us, and washed us from our sins in his own blood,

Revelation 21:5
And I saw heaven opened, and behold a white horse; and he that sat upon him was called Faithful and True, and in righteousness he doth judge and make war.

Revelation 19:11
And he that sat upon the throne said, Behold, I make all things new. And he said unto me, Write: for these words are true and faithful.

Revelation 22:6
And he said unto me, These sayings are faithful and true: and the Lord God of the holy prophets sent his angel to shew unto his servants the things which must shortly be done.

Numbers 23:19
God is not a man, that he should lie; neither the son of man, that he should repent: hath he said, and shall he not do it? or hath he spoken, and shall he not make it good?

Hebrews 13:5
Let your conversation be without covetousness; and be content with such things as ye have: for he hath said, I will never leave thee, nor forsake thee.

Psalms 121:3-4
He will not suffer thy foot to be moved: he that keepeth thee will not slumber. Behold, he that keepeth Israel shall neither slumber nor sleep.

Giving and Charity

Genesis 26:12
Then Isaac sowed in that land, and reaped in the same year a hundredfold; and the Lord blessed him.

Luke 6:38
"Give and it will be given to you. A good measure, pressed down, shaken together and running over, will be poured into your lap."

Proverbs 22:9
"A generous man will himself be blessed, for he shares his food with the poor."

Prov 11:24
There is one who scatters, yet increases more; And there is one who withholds more than is right, but it leads to poverty.

Isa 32:20
Blessed are you who sow beside all waters, Who send out freely the feet of the ox and the donkey.

Prov 28:27
He who gives to the poor will not lack, But he who hides his eyes will have many curses.

What The Bible Promises About...

2Cor 9:6
But this I say: He who sows sparingly will also reap sparingly, and he who sows bountifully will also reap bountifully.

Isa.30:21
Whether you turn to the right or to the left your ears will hear a voice behind you, Saying, "This is the way; walk in it"

Ps.48:14
For this is God, Our God forever and ever; He will be our guide, Even to death.

Ps.23:1,3
The Lord is my shepherd; I shall not want, He restores my soul; He leads me in the paths of righeousness For His name's sake.

Ps.139:9-10
If I take the wings of the morning, And dwell in the uttermost parts of the sea,10 Even there Your hand shall lead me, And Your right hand shall hold me.

Psalm 32:8
"I will instruct you and teach you in the way you should go; I will counsel you and watch over you."

Isaiah 42:16
"I will lead the blind by ways they have not known, along unfamiliar paths I will guide them, I will turn the darkness into light before them and make the rough places smooth. These are the things I will do; I will not forsake them."

Decision making

Psalm 32:8
"I will instruct you and teach you in the way you should go; I will counsel you and watch over you."

John 8:12
"When Jesus spoke again to the people, he said, "I am the light of the world. Whoever follows me will never walk in darkness, but will have the light of life."

John 14:26
"But the Counsellor, the Holy Spirit, whom the Father will send in my name, will teach you all things and will remind you of everything I have said to you."

James 1:5
"If any of you lacks wisdom, he should ask God, who gives generously to all without finding fault, and it will be given to him."

Ps.25:8-10
He guides the humble in what is right and teaches them His Way. All the ways of the Lord are loving and faithful for those who keep the demands of His covenant.

Ps.25:12-14
Who are those who fear the Lord? He will show them the path they should choose. They will live in prosperity, and their children will inherit the land.

Ps 32:8
I will instruct you and teach you in the way you should go; I will guide you with My eye.

2 Tim.3:16-17
All Scripture is given by inspiration of God, and is profitable for doctrine, for reproof, for correct ion, for instruction in righteousness, 17 that the man of God may be complete, thoroughly equipped for every good work.

Prov.15:33
The fear of the Lord is the instruction of wisdom, And before honour is humility.

Heaven

Rev.21:2
I saw the Holy City, the New Jerusalem, coming down out of Heaven from God, prepared as a bride beautifully dressed for her husband. And I heard a loud Voice from the throne saying: "Now the dwelling of God is with men, and He will live with them. They will be His people and God Himself will be with them and be their God

1 Pet.1:4-5
...to an inheritance incorruptible and undefiled and that does not fade away, reserved in heaven for you, who are kept by the power of God through faith for salvation ready to be revealed in the last time.

2 Pet.1:10-11 NKJV
Therefore, brethren, be even more diligent to make your call and election sure, for if you do these things you will never stumble; 11 for so an entrance will be supplied to you abundantly into the everlasting kingdom of our Lord and Saviour Jesus Christ.

2 Pet.3:13
Nevertheless we, according to His promise, look for new heavens and a new earth in which righteousness dwells.

Luke 23:43
And Jesus said to him, "Assuredly, I say to you, today you will be with Me in Paradise."

The second coming of Christ

John 14:2-3
In my Father's House are many rooms; if it were not so I would have told you. I am going there to prepare a place for you. And if I go and prepare a place for you I will Come back and take you to be with Me

John 14:28
You have heard Me say to you, 'I am going away and coming back to you.' If you loved Me, you would rejoice because I said, 'I am going to the Father,' for My Father is greater than I.

What The Bible Promises About...

Acts 1:11
Who also said, "Men of Galilee, why do you stand gazing up into heaven? This same Jesus, who was taken up from you into heaven, will so come in like manner as you saw Him go into heaven.

1Thess 4:16-17
For the Lord Himself will descend from heaven with a shout, with the voice of an archangel, and with the trumpet of God. And the dead in Christ will rise first. Then we who are alive and remain shall be caught up together with them in the clouds to meet the Lord in the air. And thus we shall always be with the Lord.

Col.3:4
When Christ who is our life appears, then you also will appear with Him in glory.

Heb 9:28
So Christ was offered once to bear the sins of many. To those who eagerly wait for Him He will appear a second time, apart from sin, for salvation.

Rev 1:7
Behold, He is coming with clouds, and every eye will see Him, even they who pierced Him. And all the tribes of the earth will mourn because of Him. Even so, Amen.

Justification

2 Cor.5:21
God made Him who had no sin to be sin for us, so that in Him we might become the righteousness of God.

Rom.8:10
And if Christ is in you, the body is dead because of sin, but the Spirit is life because of righteousness.

1 Cor 1:30
But of Him you are in Christ Jesus, who became for us wisdom from God – and righteousness and sanctification and redemption.

Rom.3:21-22
But now the righteousness of God apart from the law is revealed, being witnessed by the Law and the Prophets, even the righteousness of God, through faith in Jesus Christ, to all and on all who believe. For there is no difference;

Rom.4:4-5
Now to him who works, the wages are not counted as grace but as debt. But to him who does not work but believes on Him who justifies the ungodly, his faith is accounted for righteousness

Rom.5:17
For if by the one man's offense death reigned through the one, much more those who receive abundance of

grace and of the gift of righteousness will reign in life through the One, Jesus Christ.

Prayer

Rom.5:17
For the Eyes of the Lord are on the righteous and His Ears are attentive to their prayer.

Ps 34:17
The righteous cry out, and the Lord hears, And delivers them out of all their troubles.

2 Chron 16:9
For the eyes of the Lord run to and fro throughout the whole earth, to show Himself strong on behalf of those whose heart is loyal to Him. In this you have done foolishly; therefore from now on you shall have wars.

Ps.102:17
He shall regard the prayer of the destitute, And shall not despise their prayer.

Isa.65:24
It shall come to pass That before they call, I will answer; And while they are still speaking, I will hear.

Jer.33:3
Call to Me, and I will answer you, and show you great and mighty things, which you do not know.

Mark 11:24
Therefore I say to you, whatever things you ask when you pray, believe that you receive them, and you will have them.

John 16:24
Until now you have asked nothing in My name. Ask, and you will receive, that your joy may be full.

John 15:7
If you abide in Me, and My words abide in you, you will ask what you desire, and it shall be done for you.

Isa.58:9
Then you shall call, and the Lord will answer; You shall cry, and He will say, 'Here I am. If you take away the yoke from your midst, The pointing of the finger, and speaking wickedness,

Eph.3:20
Now to Him who is able to do exceedingly abundantly above all that we ask or think, according to the power that works in us,

Matt 7:7
Ask, and it will be given to you; seek, and you will find; knock, and it will be opened to you.

Jer.33:3
Call to Me, and I will answer you, and show you great and mighty things, which you do not know.

Jeremiah 29:12
Then you will call upon me and come and pray to me, and I will listen to you.

Isaiah 65:24
Before they call I will answer; while they are still speaking I will hear."

The power for God's service

Zech.4:6
This is the word of the Lord to Zerubbabel: "Not by might nor by power, but by My Spirit" says the Lord Almighty

Acts 1:8
But you shall receive power when the Holy Spirit has come upon you; and you shall be witnesses to Me in Jerusalem, and in all Judea and Samaria, and to the end of the earth."

Isa.40:31
But those who wait on the Lord Shall renew their strength; They shall mount up with wings like eagles, They shall run and not be weary, They shall walk and not faint.

Eph.6:13
Therefore take up the whole armour of God, that you may be able to withstand in the evil day, and having done all, to stand.

Phil.2:13
For it is God who works in you both to will and to do for His good pleasure.

Eph.3:16
that He would grant you, according to the riches of His glory, to be strengthened with might through His Spirit in the inner man.

Col.1:11
strengthened with all might, according to His glorious power, for all patience and longsuffering with joy.

Spiritual growth

Phil.1:6
Being confident of this, that He who began a good work in you will carry it on to completion until the day of Christ Jesus.

John 17:18-19
As You sent Me into the world, I also have sent them into the world. And for their sakes I sanctify Myself, that they also may be sanctified by the truth.

2 Peter 1:3-4
As His divine power has given to us all things that pertain to life and godliness, through the knowledge of Him who called us by glory and virtue, by which have been given to us exceedingly great and precious promises, that through these you may be partakers of the divine nature, having escaped the corruption that is in the world through lust.

2Cor.3:18
But we all, with unveiled face, beholding as in a mirror the glory of the Lord, are being transformed into the same image from glory to glory, just as by the Spirit of the Lord.

2Cor.3:18
He will keep you strong to the end so that you will be free from all blame on the day when our Lord Jesus Christ returns.

Eph 3:17-19
That Christ may dwell in your hearts through faith; that you, being rooted and grounded in love, may be able to comprehend with all the saints what is the width and length and depth and height to know the love of Christ

Phil 1:9-10
And this I pray, that your love may abound still more and more in knowledge and all discernment, that you may approve the things that are excellent, that you may be sincere and without offense till the day of Christ,

God's Wisdom

Eccl.2:26
To the man who please Him, God gives wisdom, knowledge and happiness

Prov 2:6-7
For the Lord gives wisdom; From His mouth come knowledge and understanding; He stores up sound wisdom for the upright; He is a shield to those who walk uprightly;

Prov.9:10
The fear of the Lord is the beginning of wisdom, And the knowledge of the Holy One is understanding.

Job 12:13
With Him are wisdom and strength, He has counsel and understanding.

James 1:5
But if any of you lacks wisdom, let him ask of God, who gives to all generously and without reproach, and it will be given to him.

Dan.2:20-22
Daniel answered and said: "Blessed be the name of God forever and ever, For wisdom and might are His. And He changes the times and the seasons; He removes kings and raises up kings; He gives wisdom to the wise And knowledge to those who have understanding. He reveals deep and secret things; He knows what is in the darkness, And light dwells with Him.

Isaiah 2:3
He will teach us his ways, so that we may walk in his paths.

1 Cor.1:30
But of Him you are in Christ Jesus, who became for us wisdom from God — and righteousness and sanctification and redemption.

James 1:5-7
If any of you lacks wisdom, let him ask of God, who gives to all liberally and without reproach, and it will be given to him. 6 But let him ask in faith, with no doubting, for he who doubts is like a wave of the sea driven and tossed by the wind. God's grace and favour

God's grace and favour

Genesis 12:2
And I will make of thee a great nation, and I will bless thee, and make thy name great; and thou shalt be a blessing:

Acts 4:33
And with great power gave the apostles witness of the resurrection of the Lord Jesus: and great grace was upon them all.

Proverbs 3:4
So shalt thou find favour and good understanding in the sight of God and man.

Psalms 84:11
For the Lord God is a sun and shield: the Lord will give grace and glory: no good thing will he withhold from them that walk uprightly.

Exodus 33:17
And the Lord said unto Moses, I will do this thing also that thou hast spoken: for thou hast found grace in my sight, and I know thee by name.

Job 10:12
Thou hast granted me life and favour, and thy visitation hath preserved my spirit.

Psalms 5:12
For thou, Lord, wilt bless the righteous; with favour wilt thou compass him as with a shield.

Psalms 30:7
Lord, by thy favour thou hast made my mountain to stand strong: thou didst hide thy face, and I was troubled.

Psalms 115:12-13?
The Lord hath been mindful of us: he will bless us; he will bless the house of Israel; he will bless the house of Aaron. He will bless them that fear the Lord, both small and great.

Proverbs 8:35
For whoso findeth me findeth life, and shall obtain favour of the Lord.

Proverbs 14:9
Fools make a mock at sin: but among the righteous there is favour.

What The Bible Promises About...

Proverbs 16:15
In the light of the king's countenance is life; and his favour is as a cloud of the latter rain.

Isaiah 60:10
And the sons of strangers shall build up thy walls, and their kings shall minister unto thee: for in my wrath I smote thee, but in my favour have I had mercy on thee.

2 Corinthians 4:15
For all things are for your sakes, that the abundant grace might through the thanksgiving of many redound to the glory of God.

2 Corinthians 12:9
And he said unto me, My grace is sufficient for thee: for my strength is made perfect in weakness. Most gladly therefore will I rather glory in my infirmities, that the power of Christ may rest upon me.

Ephesians 1:6
To the praise of the glory of his grace, wherein he hath made us accepted in the beloved.

Ephesians 2:8
For by grace are ye saved through faith; and that not of yourselves: it is the gift of God:

Hebrews 4:16
Let us therefore come boldly unto the throne of grace, that we may obtain mercy, and find grace to help in time of need.

Psalms 103:12-14
As far as the east is from the west, so far hath he removed our transgressions from us. Like as a father pitieth his children, so the Lord pitieth them that fear him. For he knoweth our frame; he remembereth that we are dust.

Romans 5:20
Moreover the law entered, that the offence might abound. But where sin abounded, grace did much more abound:

The truth of God's Word

John 15:26
When the Counsellor comes, whom I will send to you from the Father, the Spirit of Truth who goes out from the Father, He will testify about Me.

John 8:31-32
Then Jesus said to those Jews who believed Him, "If you abide in My word, you are My disciples indeed. And you shall know the truth, and the truth shall make you free.

Eph.5:9
For the fruit of the Spirit is in all goodness, righteousness, and truth

What The Bible Promises About...

Trusting God

Prov.3:25-26
Have no fear of sudden disaster or of the ruin that overtakes the wicked for the Lord will be your confidence and will keep your foot from being snared.

Prov.14:26
In the fear of the Lord there is strong confidence, And His children will have a place of refuge.

Isa.30:15
For thus says the Lord God, the Holy One of Israel: "In returning and rest you shall be saved; In quietness and confidence shall be your strength."

1 John 3:21
Beloved, if our heart does not condemn us, we have confidence toward God.

1John 5:14-15
Now this is the confidence that we have in Him, that if we ask anything according to His will, He hears us. And if we know that He hears us, whatever we ask, we know that we have the petitions that we have asked of Him.

<u>Proverbs 3: 5,6</u>
Trust in the Lord with all your heart and lean not on your own understanding; in all your ways ac knowledge him, and he will make your paths straight."

<u>Psalm 40:4</u>
Blessed is the man who makes the Lord his trust.

Part 4

What To Do When You feel...

Anxious

Matt.6:30,34
If that is how God clothes the grass of the field, which is here today and tomorrow is thrown into the fire, will He not much more clothe you, O you of little faith...Therefore do not worry about tomorrow, for tomorrow will worry about itself

Phil.4:6-7
Be anxious for nothing, but in everything by prayer and supplication, with thanksgiving, let your requests be made known to God; 7 and the peace of God, which surpasses all understanding, will guard your hearts and minds through Christ Jesus.

Luke 12:25-26
And which of you by worrying can add one cubit to his stature? 26 If you then are not able to do the least, why are you anxious for the rest?

1 Peter 5:6-7
Therefore humble yourselves under the mighty hand of God, that He may exalt you in due time, casting all your care upon Him, for He cares for you.

Gal.5:1
Stand fast therefore in the liberty by which Christ has made us free, and do not be entangled again with a yoke of bondage.

Matt.11:28
Come to Me, all you who labour and are heavy laden, and I will give you rest.

Condemned

Romans 8:1
There is therefore now no condemnation to them which are in Christ Jesus, who walk not after the flesh, but after the Spirit.

2 Corinthians 7:3
I speak not this to condemn you: for I have said before, that ye are in our hearts to die and live with you.

John 3:17
God sent not his Son into the world to condemn the world; but that the world through him might be saved.

John 5:24
Verily, verily, I say unto you, He that heareth my word, and believeth on him that sent me, hath everlasting life, and shall not come into condemnation; but is passed from death unto life.

Confused

<u>1 Corinthians 14:33</u>
For God is not the author of confusion, but of peace, as in all churches of the saints.

<u>2 Timothy 1:7</u>
For God hath not given us the spirit of fear; but of power, and of love, and of a sound mind.

<u>Isaiah 50:7</u>
For the Lord GOD will help me; therefore shall I not be confounded: therefore have I set my face like a flint, and I know that I shall not be ashamed.

<u>James 1:5</u>
If any of you lack wisdom, let him ask of God, that giveth to all men liberally, and upbraideth not; and it shall be given him.

<u>Proverbs 3:5-6</u>
Trust in the Lord with all thine heart; and lean not unto thine own understanding. In all thy ways acknowledge him, and he shall direct thy paths.

<u>Psalms 32:8</u>
I will instruct thee and teach thee in the way which thou shalt go: I will guide thee with mine eye

Psalms 119:165
Great peace have they which love thy law: and nothing shall offend them.

Psalms 55:22
Cast thy burden upon the Lord, and he shall sustain thee: he shall never suffer the righteous to be moved.

Isaiah 43:2
When thou passest through the waters, I will be with thee; and through the rivers, they shall not overflow thee: when thou walkest through the fire, thou shalt not be burned; neither shall the flame kindle upon thee.

Isaiah 40:29
He giveth power to the faint; and to them that have no might he increaseth strength.

Depressed

Ps.43:5
Why are you downcast O my soul? Why so disturbed within me? Put your hope in God, for I will yet praise Him my Saviour and my God.

Ps 73:26
My flesh and my heart fail; But God is the strength of my heart and my portion forever.

Ps.37:23-24
The steps of a good man are ordered by the Lord, And He delights in his way. Though he fall, he shall not be utterly cast down; For the Lord upholds him with His hand.

Ps.34:4-7
The angel of the Lord encamps all around those who fear, Him And delivers them.

Isa.49:15
Can a woman forget her nursing child, And not have compassion on the son of her womb? Surely they may forget, Yet I will not forget you.

Heb.13:5
Let your conduct be without covetousness; be content with such things as you have. For He Him self has said, "I will never leave you nor forsake you."

Hopeless

Psalms 30:5
For his anger endureth but a moment; in his favour is life: weeping may endure for a night, but joy cometh in the morning.

Rom.15:4
For everything that was written in the past was written to teach us so that through endurance and

the encouragement of the Scriptures we might have hope

Col.1:27
To them God willed to make known what are the riches of the glory of this mystery among the Gentiles: which is Christ in you, the hope of glory.

1 Peter 1:3
Blessed be the God and Father of our Lord Jesus Christ, who according to His abundant mercy has begotten us again to a living hope through the resurrection of Jesus Christ from the dead.

Heb.6:18-19
...that by two immutable things, in which it is impossible for God to lie, we might have strong consolation, who have fled for refuge to lay hold of the hope set before us. This hope we have as an anchor of the soul, both sure and steadfast, and which enters the Presence behind the veil,

Rom.5:2
through whom also we have access by faith into this grace in which we stand, and rejoice in hope of the glory of God.

Rom 15:13
Now may the God of hope fill you with all joy and peace in believing, that you may abound in hope by the power of the Holy Spirit.

Lonely

Hebrews 13:5
Let your conversation be without covetousness; and be content with such things as ye have: for he hath said, I will never leave thee, nor forsake thee.

Matthew 28:20
Teaching them to observe all things whatsoever I have commanded you: and, lo, I am with you always, even unto the end of the world. Amen.

1 Samuel 12:22
For the Lord will not forsake his people for his great name's sake: because it hath pleased the Lord to make you his people.

Isaiah 41:10
Fear thou not; for I am with thee: be not dismayed; for I am thy God: I will strengthen thee; yea, I will help thee; yea, I will uphold thee with the right hand of my righteousness.

John 14:18
I will not leave you comfortless: I will come to you.

John 14:1
Let not your heart be troubled: ye believe in God, believe also in me.

Deuteronomy 33:27
The eternal God is thy refuge, and underneath are the everlasting arms: and he shall thrust out the enemy from before thee; and shall say, Destroy them.

What The Bible Promises About...

Deuteronomy 4:31
(For the Lord thy God is a merciful God;) he will not forsake thee, neither destroy thee, nor forget the covenant of thy fathers which he sware unto them.

Deuteronomy 31:6
Be strong and of a good courage, fear not, nor be afraid of them: for the Lord thy God, he it is that doth go with thee; he will not fail thee, nor forsake thee.

Psalms 27:10
When my father and my mother forsake me, then the Lord will take me up.

Isaiah 54:10
For the mountains shall depart, and the hills be removed; but my kindness shall not depart from thee, neither shall the covenant of my peace be removed, saith the Lord that hath mercy on thee.

Psalms 46:1
God is our refuge and strength, a very present help in trouble.

1 Peter 5:7
Casting all your care upon him; for he careth for you.

Part 5

What To Do When You Are...

What To Do When You Are...

Experiencing sufferings, difficulties and attacks from people

Ps.37:39-40
The salvation of the righteous comes from the Lord; He is their stronghold in time of trouble. The Lord helps them and delivers them; He delivers them from the wicked and saves them because they take refuge in Him.

James 1:12
Blessed is the man who endures temptation; for when he has been approved, he will receive the crown of life which the Lord has promised to those who love Him.

Rom.5:3
And not only that, but we also glory in tribulations, knowing that tribulation produces perseverance.

1Pet.1:3-7
Blessed be the God and Father of our Lord Jesus Christ, who according to His abundant mercy has begotten us again to a living hope through the resurrection of Jesus Christ from the dead, to an inheritance incorruptible and undefiled and that does not fade away, reserved in heaven for you, who are kept by the power of God through faith for salvation ready to be revealed in the last time. In this you greatly rejoice, though now for a little while, if need be, you have been grieved by various trials,

that the genuineness of your faith, being much more precious than gold that perishes, though it is tested by fire, may be found to praise, honour, and glory at the revelation of Jesus Christ,

Jer 15:21
 will deliver you from the hand of the wicked, And I will redeem you from the grip of the terrible.

Ps 27:1-2
The Lord is my light and my salvation; Whom shall I fear? The Lord is the strength of my life; Of whom shall I be afraid? When the wicked came against me to eat up my flesh, My enemies and foes, they stumbled and fell.

1Peter 3:9
Not returning evil for evil or reviling for reviling, but on the contrary blessing, knowing that you were called to this, that you may inherit a blessing.

Rom 8:31
What then shall we say to these things? If God is for us, who can be against us?

Ex.14:13-14
And Moses said to the people, "Do not be afraid. Stand still, and see the salvation of the Lord, which He will accomplish for you today. For the Egyptians whom you see today, you shall see again no more forever.

Blessed are those who are persecuted for righteousness' sake, For theirs is the kingdom of heaven Blessed are you when they revile and persecute you, and say all kinds of evil against you falsely for My sake. Rejoice and be exceedingly glad, for great is your reward in heaven, for so they persecuted the prophets who were before you.

Luke 21:12-15
But before all these things, they will lay their hands on you and persecute you, delivering you up to the synagogues and prisons. You will be brought before kings and rulers for My name's sake. But it will turn out for you as an occasion for testimony. Therefore settle it in your hearts not to meditate beforehand on what you will answer; for I will give you a mouth and wisdom which all your adversaries will not be able to contradict or resist.

Rev. 2:10
Do not fear any of those things which you are about to suffer. Indeed, the devil is about to throw some of you into prison, that you may be tested, and you will have tribulation ten days. Be faithful until death, and I will give you the crown of life.

Experiencing temptation and demonic attacks

1 Cor.10:13
No temptation has seized you except what is common to man. And God is Faithful; He will not let you be tempted beyond what you can bear. But when are tempted, He will also provide a way out so that you can stand up under it

2 Pet.2:9
Then the Lord knows how to deliver the godly out of temptations and to reserve the unjust under punishment for the day of judgment,

Heb.4:14-16
Seeing then that we have a great High Priest who has passed through the heavens, Jesus the Son of God, let us hold fast our confession. For we do not have a High Priest who cannot sympathize with our weaknesses, but was in all points tempted as we are, yet without sin. Let us therefore come boldly to the throne of grace, that we may obtain mercy and find grace to help in time of need.

James 4:7
Therefore submit to God. Resist the devil and he will flee from you.

What To Do When You Are...

Gal. 1:3-4
Grace to you and peace from God the Father and our Lord Jesus Christ, who gave Himself for our sins, that He might deliver us from this present evil age, according to the will of our God and Father.

Rom. 16:20
And the God of peace will crush Satan under your feet shortly.

John 16:33
These things I have spoken to you, that in Me you may have peace. In the world you will have tribulation; but be of good cheer, I have overcome the world.

1John 4:4
You are of God, little children, and have overcome them, because He who is in you is greater than he who is in the world.

Jude 1:24-25
Now unto him that is able to keep you from falling, and to present you faultless before the presence of his glory with exceeding joy, To the only wise God our Saviour, be glory and majesty, dominion and power, both now and ever. Amen.

1 Peter 1:6-7
Wherein ye greatly rejoice, though now for a season, if need be, ye are in heaviness through manifold temptations: That the trial of your faith, being much more precious than of gold that perisheth, though it

be tried with fire, might be found unto praise and honour and glory at the appearing of Jesus Christ:

James 1:2-3,12
My brethren, count it all joy when ye fall into divers temptations; Knowing this, that the trying of your faith worketh patience. Blessed is the man that endureth temptation: for when he is tried, he shall receive the crown of life, which the Lord hath promised to them that love him.

Proverbs 28:13
He that covereth his sins shall not prosper: but whoso confesseth and forsaketh them shall have mercy.

1 John 1:9
If we confess our sins, he is faithful and just to forgive us our sins, and to cleanse us from all unrighteousness.

Romans 6:14
For sin shall not have dominion over you: for ye are not under the law, but under grace.

Psalms 119:11
Thy word have I hid in mine heart, that I might not sin against thee.

1 Peter 5:8-9
Be sober, be vigilant; because your adversary the devil, as a roaring lion, walketh about, seeking whom he may devour: Whom resist steadfast in the faith,

knowing that the same afflictions are accomplished in your brethren that are in the world.

Ephesians 6:10-11
Finally, my brethren, be strong in the Lord, and in the power of his might. Put on the whole armour of God, that ye may be able to stand against the wiles of the devil. Above all, taking the shield of faith, wherewith ye shall be able to quench all the fiery darts of the wicked.

Having marital problems

Ephesians 4:31-32
Let all bitterness, and wrath, and anger, and clamour, and evil speaking, be put away from you, with all malice: And be ye kind one to another, tenderhearted, forgiving one another, even as God for Christ's sake hath forgiven you.

Ephesians 5:21-33
Submitting yourselves one to another in the fear of God. Wives, submit yourselves unto your own husbands, as unto the Lord. For the husband is the head of the wife, even as Christ is the head of the church: and he is the saviour of the body. Therefore as the church is subject unto Christ, so let the wives be to their own husbands in every thing. Husbands, love your wives, even as Christ also loved the church, and gave himself for it; That he might sanctify and cleanse it with the washing of water by the word, That he might present it to himself a glorious church,

not having spot, or wrinkle, or any such thing; but that it should be holy and without blemish. So ought men to love their wives as their own bodies. He that loveth his wife loveth himself. For no man ever yet hated his own flesh; but nourisheth and cherisheth it, even as the Lord the church: For we are members of his body, of his flesh, and of his bones. For this cause shall a man leave his father and mother, and shall be joined unto his wife, and they two shall be one flesh. This is a great mystery: but I speak concerning Christ and the church. Nevertheless let every one of you in particular so love his wife even as himself; and the wife see that she reverence her husband.

1 Peter 3:1-7
Likewise, ye wives, be in subjection to your own husbands; that, if any obey not the word, they also may without the word be won by the conversation of the wives; While they behold your chaste conversation coupled with fear. Whose adorning let it not be that outward adorning of plaiting the hair, and of wearing of gold, or of putting on of apparel; But let it be the hidden man of the heart, in that which is not corruptible, even the ornament of a meek and quiet spirit, which is in the sight of God of great price. For after this manner in the old time the holy women also, who trusted in God, adorned themselves, being in subjection unto their own husbands: Even as Sara obeyed Abraham, calling him lord: whose daughters ye are, as long as ye do well, and are not afraid with any amazement. Likewise, ye husbands, dwell with them according

to knowledge, giving honour unto the wife, as unto the weaker vessel, and as being heirs together of the grace of life; that your prayers be not hindered.

Genesis 2:18
And the Lord God said, It is not good that the man should be alone; I will make him an help meet for him.

Genesis 2:24
Therefore shall a man leave his father and his mother, and shall cleave unto his wife: and they shall be one flesh.

Romans 13:10
Love worketh no ill to his neighbour: therefore love is the fulfilling of the law.

1 Peter 3:8-11
Finally, be ye all of one mind, having compassion one of another, love as brethren, be pitiful, be courteous: Not rendering evil for evil, or railing for railing: but contrariwise blessing; knowing that ye are thereunto called, that ye should inherit a blessing. For he that will love life, and see good days, let him refrain his tongue from evil, and his lips that they speak no guile: Let him eschew evil, and do good; let him seek peace, and ensue it.

Proverbs 3:5-6
Trust in the Lord with all thine heart; and lean not unto thine own understanding. In all thy ways acknowledge him, and he shall direct thy paths.

Proverbs 10:12
Hatred stirreth up strifes: but love covereth all sins.

Psalms 101:2
I will behave myself wisely in a perfect way. O when wilt thou come unto me? I will walk within my house with a perfect heart.

1 Peter 1:22
Seeing ye have purified your souls in obeying the truth through the Spirit unto unfeigned love of the brethren, see that ye love one another with a pure heart fervently:

In Financial Crisis

Psalms 23:1
The Lord is my shepherd; I shall not want.

Psalms 34:10
The young lions do lack, and suffer hunger: but they that seek the Lord shall not want any good thing.

Psalms 37:25
I have been young, and now am old; yet have I not seen the righteous forsaken, nor his seed begging bread.

3 John 1:2
Beloved, I wish above all things that thou mayest prosper and be in health, even as thy soul prospereth.

Deuteronomy 28:2-8

And all these blessings shall come on thee, and overtake thee, if thou shalt hearken unto the voice of the Lord thy God. Blessed shalt thou be in the city, and blessed shalt thou be in the field. Blessed shall be the fruit of thy body, and the fruit of thy ground, and the fruit of thy cattle, the increase of thy kine, and the flocks of thy sheep. Blessed shall be thy basket and thy store. Blessed shalt thou be when thou comest in, and blessed shalt thou be when thou goest out. The Lord shall cause thine enemies that rise up against thee to be smitten before thy face: they shall come out against thee one way, and flee before thee seven ways. The Lord shall command the blessing upon thee in thy storehouses, and in all that thou settest thine hand unto; and he shall bless thee in the land which the Lord thy God giveth thee.

Deuteronomy 28:11-13

And the Lord shall make thee plenteous in goods, in the fruit of thy body, and in the fruit of thy cattle, and in the fruit of thy ground, in the land which the Lord sware unto thy fathers to give thee. The Lord shall open unto thee his good treasure, the heaven to give the rain unto thy land in his season, and to bless all the work of thine hand: and thou shalt lend unto many nations, and thou shalt not borrow. And the Lord shall make thee the head, and not the tail; and thou shalt be above only, and thou shalt not be beneath; if that thou hearken unto the commandments of the Lord thy God, which I command thee this day, to observe and to do them:

Joshua 1:8
This book of the law shall not depart out of thy mouth; but thou shalt meditate therein day and night, that thou mayest observe to do according to all that is written therein: for then thou shalt make thy way prosperous, and then thou shalt have good success.

2 Corinthians 9:6-8
But this I say, He which soweth sparingly shall reap also sparingly; and he which soweth bountifully shall reap also bountifully. Every man according as he purposeth in his heart, so let him give; not grudgingly, or of necessity: for God loveth a cheerful giver. And God is able to make all grace abound toward you; that ye, always having all sufficiency in all things, may abound to every good work:

Philippians 4:19
But my God shall supply all your need according to his riches in glory by Christ Jesus.

Deuteronomy 8:7-14,18
For the Lord thy God bringeth thee into a good land, a land of brooks of water, of fountains and depths that spring out of valleys and hills; A land of wheat, and barley, and vines, and fig trees, and pomegranates; a land of oil olive, and honey; A land wherein thou shalt eat bread without scarceness, thou shalt not lack any thing in it; a land whose stones are iron, and out of whose hills thou mayest dig brass. When thou hast eaten and art full, then thou shalt bless

the Lord thy God for the good land which he hath given thee. Beware that thou forget not the Lord thy God, in not keeping his commandments, and his judgments, and his statutes, which I command thee this day: Lest when thou hast eaten and art full, and hast built goodly houses, and dwelt therein; And when thy herds and thy flocks multiply, and thy silver and thy gold is multiplied, and all that thou hast is multiplied; Then thine heart be lifted up, and thou forget the Lord thy God, which brought thee forth out of the land of Egypt, from the house of bondage; But thou shalt remember the Lord thy God: for it is he that giveth thee power to get wealth, that he may establish his covenant which he sware unto thy fathers, as it is this day.

Malachi 3:10-12
Bring ye all the tithes into the storehouse, that there may be meat in mine house, and prove me now herewith, saith the Lord of hosts, if I will not open you the windows of heaven, and pour you out a blessing, that there shall not be room enough to receive it. And I will rebuke the devourer for your sakes, and he shall not destroy the fruits of your ground; neither shall your vine cast her fruit before the time in the field, saith the Lord of hosts. And all nations shall call you blessed: for ye shall be a delightsome land, saith the Lord of hosts.

In times of fear and doubt

2 Tim 1:7-8
For God has not given us a spirit of fear, but of power and of love and of a sound mind.

Genesis 28:15
"I am with you and will watch over you wherever you go, and I will bring you back to this land. I will not leave you until I have done what I have promised you."

Deuteronomy 31:8
"The Lord himself goes before you and will be with you; he will never leave you nor forsake you. Do not be afraid; do not be discouraged."

Psalm 50:15
"and call upon me in the day of trouble; I will deliver you, and you will honour me."

Ps 112:6b-7
Those who are righteous will be long remembered. They do not fear bad news; they confidently trust the Lord to care for them.

Prov 3:24-26
You can go to bed without fear; you will lie down and sleep soundly. You need not be afraid of sudden disaster or the destruction that comes upon the wicked, for the Lord is your security. He will keep your foot from being caught in a trap.

What To Do When You Are...

Luke 12:4-5
"Dear friends, don't be afraid of those who want to kill your body; they cannot do any more to you after that. But I'll tell you whom to fear. Fear God, who has the power to kill you and then throw you into hell. Yes, he's the one to fear.

Prov 28:1
The wicked flee when no one pursues, But the righteous are bold as a lion.

Luke 21:17-18
"All men will hate you because of me. But not a hair of your head will perish."

James 4:8
"Come near to God and he will come near to you."

Isa.41:10
So do not fear for I am with you; do not be dismayed for I am your God. I will Strengthen you and help you; I will uphold you with My Righteous right hand.

Isa 41:13
For I, the Lord your God, will hold your right hand, Saying to you, 'Fear not, I will help you.'

Isa.43:1 NKJV
But now, thus says the Lord, who created you, O Jacob, And He who formed you, O Israel: "Fear not, for I have redeemed you; I have called you by your name; You are Mine.

2 Tim. 1:7
For God has not given us a spirit of fear, but of power and of love and of a sound mind.

Luke 12:6-7
"Are not five sparrows sold for two copper coins? And not one of them is forgotten before God. But the very hairs of your head are all numbered. Do not fear therefore; you are of more value than many sparrows.

1 John 4:18
There is no fear in love; but perfect love casts out fear, because fear involves torment. But he who fears has not been made perfect in love.

Rom. 4:21
And being fully convinced that what He had promised He was also able to perform.

Ps. 112:7
He will not be afraid of evil tidings; His heart is steadfast, trusting in the Lord.

Isa. 58:9
Then you shall call, and the Lord will answer; You shall cry, and He will say, 'Here I am.' If you take away the yoke from your midst, The pointing of the finger, and speaking wickedness.

What To Do When You Are...

Waiting on God

Psalms 27:14
Wait on the Lord: be of good courage, and he shall strengthen thine heart: wait, I say, on the Lord.

Psalms 33:20
Our soul waiteth for the Lord: he is our help and our shield.

Psalms 62:5
My soul, wait thou only upon God; for my expectation is from him.

Psalms 130:5
I wait for the Lord, my soul doth wait, and in his word do I hope.

Psalms 145:15-16
The eyes of all wait upon thee; and thou givest them their meat in due season. Thou openest thine hand, and satisfiest the desire of every living thing.

Isaiah 25:9
And it shall be said in that day, Lo, this is our God; we have waited for him, and he will save us: this is the Lord; we have waited for him, we will be glad and rejoice in his salvation.

Isaiah 40:31
But they that wait upon the Lord shall renew their strength; they shall mount up with wings as eagles; they

shall run, and not be weary; and they shall walk, and not faint.

Habakkuk 2:3
For the vision is yet for an appointed time, but at the end it shall speak, and not lie: though it tarry, wait for it; because it will surely come, it will not tarry.

Hebrews 3:14
For we are made partakers of Christ, if we hold the beginning of our confidence steadfast unto the end;

Hebrews 10:23
Let us hold fast the profession of our faith without wavering; (for he is faithful that promised;

Part 6

What To Do When You Need...

Comfort

Ps 46:1
God is our refuge and strength, A very present help in trouble.

Matt.5:4
Blessed are those who mourn for they will be comforted

2 Cor.1:3-4
Blessed be the God and Father of our Lord Jesus Christ, the Father of mercies and God of all comfort, who comforts us in all our tribulation, that we may be able to comfort those who are in any trouble, with the comfort with which we ourselves are comforted by God.

2Thess.2:16-17
Now may our Lord Jesus Christ Himself, and our God and Father, who has loved us and given us everlasting consolation and good hope by grace, comfort your hearts and establish you in every good word and work.

Isa.49:13
Sing, O heavens! Be joyful, O earth! And break out in singing, O mountains! For the Lord has comforted His people, And will have mercy on His afflicted.

John 14:18 -
I will not leave you orphans; I will come to you.

What To Do When You Need...

John 16:33
"I have told you these things, so that in me you may have peace. In this world you will have trouble. But take heart! I have overcome the world! "

Matt. 11:28
"Come to me, all you who are weary and burdened, and I will give you rest."

Isa 40:1
"Comfort, comfort my people," says your God.

Isa 51:3
The Lord will comfort Israel again and have pity on her ruins. Her desert will blossom like Eden, her barren wilderness like the garden of the Lord. Joy and gladness will be found there. Songs of thanksgiving will fill the air.

2 Timothy 1:7
For God hath not given us the spirit of fear; but of power, and of love, and of a sound mind.

1 Corinthians 14:33
For God is not the author of confusion, but of peace, as in all churches of the saints

Isaiah 50:7
For the Lord GOD will help me; therefore shall I not be confounded: therefore have I set my face like a flint, and I know that I shall not be ashamed.

Psalms 55:22
Cast thy burden upon the Lord, and he shall sustain thee: he shall never suffer the righteous to be moved.

Philippians 4:6-7
Be careful for nothing; but in every thing by prayer and supplication with thanksgiving let your requests be made known unto God. And the peace of God, which passeth all understanding, shall keep your hearts and minds through Christ Jesus.

Philippians 4:8
Finally, brethren, whatsoever things are true, whatsoever things are honest, whatsoever things are just, whatsoever things are pure, whatsoever things are lovely, whatsoever things are of good report; if there be any virtue, and if there be any praise, think on these things.

2 Corinthians 1:3-4
Blessed be God, even the Father of our Lord Jesus Christ, the Father of mercies, and the God of all comfort; Who comforteth us in all our tribulation, that we may be able to comfort them which are in any trouble, by the comfort wherewith we ourselves are comforted of God.

Courage

Isaiah 40:29
"He gives strength to the weary and increases the power of the weak"

Isaiah 43:1
"Fear not, for I have redeemed you; I have summoned you by name; you are mine"

What To Do When You Need...

Isaiah 43:2
When thou passest through the waters, I will be with thee; and through the rivers, they shall not overflow thee: when thou walkest through the fire, thou shalt not be burned; neither shall the flame kindle upon thee.

Isaiah 41:10
Fear thou not; for I am with thee: be not dismayed; for I am thy God: I will strengthen thee; yea, I will help thee; yea, I will uphold thee with the right hand of my righteousness.

Isaiah 40:31
But they that wait upon the Lord shall renew their strength; they shall mount up with wings as eagles; they shall run, and not be weary; and they shall walk, and not faint.

Deut 31:5-6
Be strong and of good courage, do not fear nor be afraid of them; for the Lord your God, He is the One who goes with you. He will not leave you nor forsake you."

Josh 1:9
Have I not commanded you? Be strong and of good courage; do not be afraid, nor be dismayed, for the Lord your God is with you wherever you go."

Inspiration

Philippians 4:8,13
Finally, brethren, whatsoever things are true, whatsoever things are honest, whatsoever things are just, whatsoever things are pure, whatsoever things are lovely, whatsoever things are of good report; if there be any virtue, and if there be any praise, think on these things...I can do all things through Christ which strengtheneth me.

Luke 12:12
For the Holy Ghost shall teach you in the same hour what ye ought to say.

Proverbs 20:27
The spirit of man is the candle of the Lord, searching all the inward parts of the belly.

Psalms 119:92
Unless thy law had been my delights, I should then have perished in mine affliction.

Psalms 119:105
Thy word is a lamp unto my feet, and a light unto my path.

Job 32:8
But there is a spirit in man: and the inspiration of the Almighty giveth them understanding.

What To Do When You Need...

Joy

John 15:11
I have told you this so that My joy may be in you and that your joy may be complete.

Ps 16:11
You will show me the path of life; In Your presence is fullness of joy; At Your right hand are pleasures forevermore.

Joel 2:23
Be glad then, ye children of Zion, and rejoice in the Lord your God: for he hath given you the former rain moderately, and he will cause to come down for you the rain, the former rain, and the latter rain in the first month.

Psalms 118:24
This is the day which the Lord hath made; we will rejoice and be glad in it.

Rom 14:17
for the kingdom of God is not eating and drinking, but righteousness and peace and joy in the Holy Spirit.

Isa 55:12
"For you shall go out with joy, And be led out with peace; The mountains and the hills shall break forth into singing before you, And all the trees of the field shall clap their hands.

Isa 35:10
And the ransomed of the Lord shall return, And come to Zion with singing, With everlasting joy on their heads. They shall obtain joy and gladness, And sorrow and sighing shall flee away.

John 16:22
"...but I will see you again and you will rejoice, and no one will take away your joy."

2Chron.20:17
Then they returned, every man of Judah and Jerusalem, and Jehoshaphat in the forefront of them, to go again to Jerusalem with joy; for the Lord had made them to rejoice over their enemies.

Ezra 6:22
And kept the feast of unleavened bread seven days with joy: for the Lord had made them joyful, and turned the heart of the king of Assyria unto them, to strengthen their hands in the work of the house of God, the God of Israel.

Neh.8:10
Then he said unto them, Go your way, eat the fat, and drink the sweet, and send portions unto them for whom nothing is prepared: for this day is holy unto our Lord: neither be ye sorry; for the joy of the Lord is your strength.

Neh.12:43
Also that day they offered great sacrifices, and rejoiced: for God had made them rejoice with great joy: the

wives also and the children rejoiced: so that the joy of Jerusalem was heard even afar off"

Psa.5:11
But let all those that put their trust in thee rejoice: let them ever shout for joy, because thou defendest them: let them also that love thy name be joyful in thee.

Psa. 21:1
The king shall joy in thy strength, O Lord; and in thy salvation how greatly shall he rejoice

Psa.43:4
Then will I go unto the altar of God, unto God my exceeding joy: yea, upon the harp will I praise thee, O God my God"

Psa.105:43
And he brought forth his people with joy, and his chosen with gladness

Isaiah 12:3
Therefore with joy shall ye draw water out of the wells of salvation.

Isaiah 51:11
Therefore the redeemed of the Lord shall return, and come with singing unto Zion; and everlasting joy shall be upon their head: they shall obtain gladness and joy; and sorrow and mourning shall flee away.

Isa.35:10
And the ransomed of the Lord shall return, and come to Zion with songs and everlasting joy upon their heads: they shall obtain joy and gladness, and sorrow and sighing shall flee away.

Isa.51:3
For the Lord shall comfort Zion: he will comfort all her waste places; and he will make her wilderness like Eden, and her desert like the garden of the Lord; joy and gladness shall be found therein, thanksgiving, and the voice of melody

Isa.53:11
Therefore the redeemed of the Lord shall return, and come with singing unto Zion; and everlasting joy shall be upon their head: they shall obtain gladness and joy; and sorrow and mourning shall flee away

Isaiah 60:15
Whereas thou hast been forsaken and hated, so that no man went through thee, I will make thee an eternal excellency, a joy of many generations.

Isaiah 61:3,7
To appoint unto them that mourn in Zion, to give unto them beauty for ashes, the oil of joy for mourning, the garment of praise for the spirit of heaviness; that they might be called trees of righteousness, the planting of the Lord, that he might be glorified. For your shame ye shall have double; and for confusion they shall rejoice in their portion: therefore in their land they shall possess the double: everlasting joy shall be unto them.

What To Do When You Need...

Isaiah 65:14
Behold, my servants shall sing for joy of heart, but ye shall cry for sorrow of heart, and shall howl for vexation of spirit.

Isaiah 65:19
And I will rejoice in Jerusalem, and joy in my people: and the voice of weeping shall be no more heard in her, nor the voice of crying.

1 Peter 1:8
Whom having not seen, ye love; in whom, though now ye see him not, yet believing, ye rejoice with joy unspeakable and full of glory:

1 Peter 4:13
But rejoice, inasmuch as ye are partakers of Christ's sufferings; that, when his glory shall be revealed, ye may be glad also with exceeding joy.

1 Thessalonians 2:20
For ye are our glory and joy.

Galatians 5:22
But the fruit of the Spirit is love, joy, peace, longsuffering, gentleness, goodness, faith.

Romans 14:17
For the kingdom of God is not meat and drink; but righteousness, and peace, and joy in the Holy Ghost.

John 17:13
And now come I to thee; and these things I speak in the world, that they might have my joy fulfilled in themselves.

Zechariah 8:19
Thus saith the Lord of hosts; The fast of the fourth month, and the fast of the fifth, and the fast of the seventh, and the fast of the tenth, shall be to the house of Judah joy and gladness, and cheerful feasts; therefore love the truth and peace.

Luke 2:10
And the angel said unto them, Fear not: for, behold, I bring you good tidings of great joy, which shall be to all people.

John 15:11
These things have I spoken unto you, that my joy might remain in you, and that your joy might be full.

John 16:20
Verily, verily, I say unto you, That ye shall weep and lament, but the world shall rejoice: and ye shall be sorrowful, but your sorrow shall be turned into joy. John 16:22 And ye now therefore have sorrow: but I will see you again, and your heart shall rejoice, and your joy no man taketh from you.

Jeremiah 15:16
Thy words were found, and I did eat them; and thy word was unto me the joy and rejoicing of mine heart: for I am called by thy name, O Lord God of hosts.

Jeremiah 31:13
Then shall the virgin rejoice in the dance, both young men and old together: for I will turn their mourning into joy, and will comfort them, and make them rejoice from their sorrow.

Psalms 30:5
For his anger endureth but a moment; in his favour is life: weeping may endure for a night, but joy cometh in the morning.

Strength

Isa.40:29
He gives strength to the weary and increases the power of the weak.

Ps.29:11
The Lord will give strength to His people; The Lord will bless His people with peace.

Isa.26:4
Trust in the Lord forever, For in Yah, the Lord, is everlasting strength.

Neh.8:10
Then he said to them, "Go your way, eat the fat, drink the sweet, and send portions to those for whom nothing is prepared; for this day is holy to our Lord. Do not sorrow, for the joy of the Lord is your strength.

Eph.6:10
Finally, my brethren, be strong in the Lord and in the power of His might.

Phil.4:13
I can do all things through Christ who strengthens me.

Isa.58:11
The Lord will guide you continually, And satisfy your soul in drought, And strengthen your bones; You shall be like a watered garden, And like a spring of water, whose waters do not fail.

What To Do When You Need...

Part 7

God's Promise Concerning...

Abundance

Deuteronomy 15:6-7
For the Lord thy God blesseth thee, as he promised thee: and thou shalt lend unto many nations, but thou shalt not borrow; and thou shalt reign over many nations, but they shall not reign over thee. If there be among you a poor man of one of thy brethren within any of thy gates in thy land which the Lord thy God giveth thee, thou shalt not harden thine heart, nor shut thine hand from thy poor brother:

Deuteronomy 30:9
And the Lord thy God will make thee plenteous in every work of thine hand, in the fruit of thy body, and in the fruit of thy cattle, and in the fruit of thy land, for good: for the Lord will again rejoice over thee for good, as he rejoiced over thy fathers:

Psalms 92:12
The righteous shall flourish like the palm tree: he shall grow like a cedar in Lebanon.

Isaiah 41:18
I will open rivers in high places, and fountains in the midst of the valleys: I will make the wilderness a pool of water, and the dry land springs of water.

Malachi 3:10
Bring ye all the tithes into the storehouse, that there may be meat in mine house, and prove me now herewith, saith the Lord of hosts, if I will not open you the windows of

heaven, and pour you out a blessing, that there shall not be room enough to receive it.

Eternal life

John 3:16
For God so loved the World that He gave His One and Only Son, that whoever believes in Him shall not perish but have eternal Life.

1 John 2:25
And this is the promise that He has promised us — eternal life.

Rom.6:23
For the wages of sin is death, but the gift of God is eternal life in Christ Jesus our Lord.

John 10:27-28
*My sheep hear My voice, and I know them, and they follow Me. 28 And I give them eternal life,
and they shall never perish; neither shall anyone snatch them out of My hand.*

John 5:24
"I tell you the truth, those who listen to my message and believe in God who sent me have eternal life. They will never be condemned for their sins, but they have already passed from death into life.

1 John 5:11-13
"I tell you the truth, those who listen to my message and believe in God who sent me have eternal life. They will never be condemned for their sins, but they have already passed from death into life.

1 John 5:11-13
And this is the testimony: that God has given us eternal life, and this life is in His Son. He who has the Son has life; he who does not have the Son of God does not have life. These things I have written to you who believe in the name of the Son of God, that you may know that you have eternal life, and that you may continue to believe in the name of the S on of God.

John 6:47
"I tell you the truth; he who believes has everlasting life."

John 11:25
"Jesus said: 'I am the resurrection and the life. He who believes in me will live, even though he dies'..."

Eternal honour

Malachi 3:17
And they shall be mine, saith the Lord of hosts, in that day when I make up my jewels; and I will spare them, as a man spareth his own son that serveth him.

James 1:12
Blessed is the man that endureth temptation: for when he is tried, he shall receive the crown of life, which the Lord hath promised to them that love him.

1 Peter 1:4
To an inheritance incorruptible, and undefiled, and that fadeth not away, reserved in heaven for you,

God's Promise Concerning...

Revelation 3:12
Him that overcometh will I make a pillar in the temple of my God, and he shall go no more out: and I will write upon him the name of my God, and the name of the city of my God, which is new Jerusalem, which cometh down out of heaven from my God: and I will write upon him my new name.

Revelation 3:21
To him that overcometh will I grant to sit with me in my throne, even as I also overcame, and am set down with my Father in his throne.

Revelation 21:7
He that overcometh shall inherit all things; and I will be his God, and he shall be my son.

Family

Prov.3:33
The Lord blesses the house of the righteous.

Prov 12:7
The wicked are overthrown and are no more, But the house of the righteous will stand.

Deut.12:28
Observe and obey all these words which I command you, that it may go well with you and your children after you forever, when you do what is good and right in the sight of the Lord your God.

Deut 28:4
Your children and your crops will be blessed.

Isa.54:13
All your children shall be taught by the Lord, And great shall be the peace of your children.

Ps.112:1-3
Praise the Lord! Blessed is the man who fears the Lord, Who delights greatly in His commandments. His descendants will be mighty on earth; The generation of the upright will be blessed. Wealth and riches will be in his house, And his righteousness endures forever.

Prov.22:6
Train up a child in the way he should go, And when he is old he will not depart from it.

Ps.128:1,3
Blessed is every one who fears the Lord, Who walks in His ways. When you eat the labour of your hands, You shall be happy, and it shall be well with you. Your wife shall be like a fruitful vine In the very heart of your house, Your children like olive plants All around your table.

Deut.4:40
You shall therefore keep His statutes and His commandments which I command you today, that it may go well with you and with your children after you, and that you may prolong your days in the land which the Lord your God is giving you for all time."

God's Promise Concerning...

Eph.6:2-3
"Honor your father and mother," which is the first commandment with promise: "that it may be well with you and you may live long on the earth."

Acts 16:31
And they said, Believe on the Lord Jesus Christ, and thou shalt be saved, and thy house.

Exodus 20:12
Honour thy father and thy mother: that thy days may be long upon the land which the Lord thy God giveth thee.

1 Timothy 3:4-5
One that ruleth well his own house, having his children in subjection with all gravity; (For if a man know not how to rule his own house, how shall he take care of the church of God?)

Psalms 127:3-5
Lo, children are an heritage of the Lord: and the fruit of the womb is his reward. As arrows are in the hand of a mighty man; so are children of the youth. Happy is the man that hath his quiver full of them: they shall not be ashamed, but they shall speak with the enemies in the gate.

Proverbs 17:6
Children's children are the crown of old men; and the glory of children are their fathers.

Malachi 4:6
And he shall turn the heart of the fathers to the children, and the heart of the children to their fathers, lest I come and smite the earth with a curse.

Proverbs 29:17
Correct thy son, and he shall give thee rest; yea, he shall give delight unto thy soul.

Proverbs 13:22
A good man leaveth an inheritance to his children's children: and the wealth of the sinner is laid up for the just.

Proverbs 23:24
The father of the righteous shall greatly rejoice: and he that begetteth a wise child shall have joy of him.

Freedom

John 8:32,36
Then you will know the Truth and the Truth will set you free... So if the Son sets you free, you will be free indeed.

Rom.6:14,22
For sin shall not have dominion over you, for you are not under law but under grace. But now having been set free from sin, and having become slaves of God, you have your fruit to holiness, and the end, everlasting life.

Rom.8:1-2
There is therefore now no condemnation to those who are in Christ Jesus, who do not walk according to the flesh, but according to the Spirit. 2 For the law of the

Spirit of life in Christ Jesus has made me free from the law of sin and death.

2 Cor.3:17
Now the Lord is the Spirit; and where the Spirit of the Lord is, there is liberty.

Acts 13:38
Therefore let it be known to you, brethren, that through this Man is preached to you the forgiveness of sins;

Jeremiah 1:8
"Do not be afraid of them, for I am with you and will rescue you," declares the Lord.

Romans 8:2
Through Christ Jesus the law of the Spirit of life set me free from the law of sin and death.

2 Timothy 4:18
The Lord will rescue me from every evil attack and will bring me safely to his heavenly kingdom. To Him be glory for ever and ever. Amen.

2 Kings 17:39
Worship the Lord your God; it is He who will deliver you from the hand of all your enemies.

John 8:36
If the Son sets you free, you will be free indeed.

Galatians 5:1
It is for freedom that Christ has set us free. Stand firm, then and do not let yourselves be burdened again by a yoke of slavery.

Guidance

Psalms 119:105
Thy word is a lamp unto my feet, and a light unto my path.

Psalms 119:11
Thy word have I hid in mine heart, that I might not sin against thee.

Psalms 119:9
Wherewithal shall a young man cleanse his way? by taking heed thereto according to thy word.

Psalms 119:24
Thy testimonies also are my delight and my counsellors.

Psalms 37:23
The steps of a good man are ordered by the Lord: and he delighteth in his way.

Psalms 32:8
I will instruct thee and teach thee in the way which thou shalt go: I will guide thee with mine eye

Psalms 23:3
He restoreth my soul: he leadeth me in the paths of righteousness for his name's sake.

God's Promise Concerning...

Psalms 19:11
Moreover by them is thy servant warned: and in keeping of them there is great reward.

Proverbs 6:22-23
When thou goest, it shall lead thee; when thou sleepest, it shall keep thee; and when thou awakes it, it shall talk with thee. For the commandment is a lamp; and the law is light; and reproofs of instruction are the way of life:

Isaiah 30:21
And thine ears shall hear a word behind thee, saying, This is the way, walk ye in it, when ye turn to the right hand, and when ye turn to the left.

John 8:31
Then said Jesus to those Jews which believed on him, If ye continue in my word, then are ye my disciples indeed;

2 Timothy 3:16-17
All scripture is given by inspiration of God, and is profitable for doctrine, for reproof, for correction, for instruction in righteousness: That the man of God may be perfect, thoroughly furnished unto all good works.

Luke 1:79
To give light to them that sit in darkness and in the shadow of death, to guide our feet into the way of peace.

Joshua 1:8
This book of the law shall not depart out of thy mouth; but thou shalt meditate therein day and night, that thou mayest observe to do according to all that is written

therein: *for then thou shalt make thy way prosperous, and then thou shalt have good success.*

Psalms 25:9
The meek will he guide in judgment: and the meek will he teach his way.

Psalms 73:23-25
Nevertheless I am continually with thee: thou hast holden me by my right hand. Thou shalt guide me with thy counsel, and afterward receive me to glory. Whom have I in heaven but thee? and there is none upon earth that I desire beside thee.

Psalms 139:10-11
Even there shall thy hand lead me, and thy right hand shall hold me. If I say, Surely the darkness shall cover me; even the night shall be light about me.

Proverbs 3:6
In all thy ways acknowledge him, and he shall direct thy paths.

Isaiah 49:10
They shall not hunger nor thirst; neither shall the heat nor sun smite them: for he that hath mercy on them shall lead them, even by the springs of water shall he guide them.

God's Promise Concerning...

Health and healing

Isa.53:5
But He was wounded for our transgressions, He was bruised for our iniquities; The chastisement for our peace was upon Him, And by His stripes we are healed.

Jer.30:17
For I will restore health to you, And heal you of your wounds,' says the Lord, 'Because they called you an outcast saying: "This is Zion; No one seeks her."'

Deut. 7:12,15
"Then it shall come to pass, because you listen to these judgments, and keep and do them, that the Lord your God will keep with you the covenant and the mercy which He swore to your fathers, and the Lord will take away from you all sickness, and will afflict you with none of the terrible diseases of Egypt which you have known, but will lay them on all those who hate you.

Proverbs 4:22
For they (His Words) are life unto those that find them, and health to all their flesh.

Ps.91:5-6,10
You shall not be afraid of the terror by night, Nor of the arrow that flies by day, Nor of the pestilence that walks in darkness, Nor of the destruction that lays waste at noonday. No evil shall befall you, Nor shall any plague come near your dwelling;

Jer.33:6
Behold, I will bring it health and healing; I will heal them and reveal to them the abundance of peace and truth.

Ex.15:25-26
So he cried out to the Lord, and the Lord showed him a tree. When he cast it into the waters, the waters were made sweet. There He made a statute and an ordinance for them, and there He tested them, and said, "If you diligently heed the voice of the Lord your God and do what is right in His sight, give ear to His commandments and keep all His statutes, I will put none of the diseases on you which I have brought on the Egyptians. For I am the Lord who heals you."

Ps.103:3
Who forgives all your iniquities, Who heals all your diseases.

Mal.4:2
But to you who fear My name, The Sun of Righteousness shall arise, With healing in His wings; And you shall go out, And grow fat like stall-fed calves.

1 Pet.2:24
who Himself bore our sins in His own body on the tree, that we, having died to sins, might live or righteousness — by whose stripes you were healed.

James 5:13-14,16;
Is anyone among you suffering? Let him pray. Is anyone cheerful? Let him sing psalms. Is anyone among you sick?

Let him call for the elders of the church, and let them pray over him, anointing him with oil in the name of the Lord. Confess your trespasses to one another, and pray for one another, that you may be healed. The effective, fervent prayer of a righteous man avails much.

Matt.8:16-17
When evening had come, they brought to Him many who were demon-possessed. And He cast out the spirits with a word, and healed all who were sick, that it might be fulfilled which was spoken by Isaiah the prophet, saying:" He Himself took our infirmities And bore our sicknesses."

His presence

Ex 33:14
And He said, "My Presence will go with you, and I will give yo rest."

Matt.28:20
And surely I am with you always to the very end of the age.

Isa 43:5
Fear not, for I am with you; I will bring your descendants from the east, And gather you from the west.

James 4:8
Draw near to God and He will draw near to you. Cleanse your hands, you sinners; and purify your hearts, you double-minded.

John 14:15-16
If you love Me, keep My commandments. And I will pray the Father, and He will give you another Helper, that He may abide with you forever.

Matt. 18:20
For where two or three are gathered together in My name, I am there in the midst of them

Ps. 23:4
Yea, though I walk through the valley of the shadow of death, I will fear no evil; For You are with me; Your rod and Your staff, they comfort me.

Heb. 13:5
Let your conduct be without covetousness; be content with such things as you have. For He Himself has said, "I will never leave you nor forsake you.

His unfailing Love

Rom. 5:8
But God demonstrates His own Love for us in this: While we were still sinners, Christ died for us.

Jer. 31:3 NKJV
The Lord has appeared of old to me, saying:" Yes, I have loved you with an everlasting love; Therefore with lovingkindness I have drawn you.

Isa. 54:10 NKJV
For the mountains shall depart And the hills be removed, But My kindness shall not depart from you, Nor shall My

covenant of peace be removed," Says the Lord, who has mercy on you.

1 John 4:9-10 NKJV
In this the love of God was manifested toward us, that God has sent His only begotten Son into the world, that we might live through Him. 10 In this is love, not that we loved God, but that He loved us and sent His Son to be the propitiation for our sins.

John 15:9 NKJV
"As the Father loved Me, I also have loved you; abide in My love.

1 John 3:1 NKJV
Behold what manner of love the Father has bestowed on us, that we should be called children of God! Therefore the world does not know us, because it did not know Him.

Jeremiah 31:3
"I have loved you with an everlasting love; I have drawn you with loving-kindness."

Proverbs 8:17
"I love those who love me, and those who seek me find me."

1 Cor. 2:9
"No eye has seen, no ear has heard, no mind has conceived what God has prepared for those who love him."

His Word

2 Tim.3:16-17
All Scripture is God-Breathed and is useful for teaching, rebuking, correcting and training in righteousness so that the man of God may be thoroughly equipped for every good work

1 Pet.1:25
But the word of the Lord endures forever. Now this is the word which by the gospel was preached to you.

Isa 40:8
The grass withers, the flower fades, But the word of our God stands forever.

Matt.4:4
But He answered and said, "It is written, 'Man shall not live by bread alone, but by every word that proceeds from the mouth of God.'"

Deut.29:29
The secret things belong to the Lord our God, but those things which are revealed belong to us and to our children forever, that we may do all the words of this law.

Jos.1:8
This Book of the Law shall not depart from your mouth, but you shall meditate in it day and night, that you may observe to do according to all that is written in it. For then you will make your way prosperous, and then you will have good success.

God's Promise Concerning...

Isa.55: 10,11
For as the rain comes down, and the snow from heaven, And do not return there, But water the earth, And make it bring forth and bud, That it may give seed to the sower And bread to the eater So shall My word be that goes forth from My mouth; It shall not return to Me void, But it shall accomplish what I please, And it shall prosper in the thing for which I sent it.

Heb.4:12
For the word of God is living and powerful, and sharper than any two-edged sword, piercing even to the division of soul and spirit, and of joints and marrow, and is a discerner of the thoughts and intents of the heart.

Deut. 11:18
Fix these words of mine in your hearts and minds; tie them as symbols on your hands and bind them on your foreheads.

Psalm 119:105
Your word is a lamp to my feet and a light for my path.

Acts 20:32
Now I commit you to God and to the word of his grace, which can build you up and give you an inheritance among all those who are sanctified.

Holy Spirit

Luke 11:13
If you then, though you are evil, know how to give good gifts to your children, how much more will your Father in Heaven give The Holy Spirit to those who ask Him

Isa. 44:3
For I will pour water on him who is thirsty, And floods on the dry ground; I will pour My Spirit on your descendants, And My blessing on your offspring;

John 14:16-17
And I will pray the Father, and He will give you another Helper, that He may abide with you forever the Spirit of truth, whom the world cannot receive, because it neither sees Him nor knows Him; but you know Him, for He dwells with you and will be in you.

John 16:7
Nevertheless I tell you the truth. It is to your advantage that I go away; for if I do not go away, the Helper will not come to you; but if I depart, I will send Him to you.

Acts 1:8
But you shall receive power when the Holy Spirit has come upon you; and you shall be witnesses to Me in Jerusalem, and in all Judea and Samaria, and to the end of the earth."

Acts 2:38-39
Then Peter said to them, "Repent, and let every one of you be baptized in the name of Jesus Christ for the remission

of sins; and you shall receive the gift of the Holy Spirit. For the promise is to you and to your children, and to all who are afar off, as many as the Lord our God will call."

Gal.4:6
And because you are sons, God has sent forth the Spirit of His Son into your hearts, crying out, "Abba, Father!"

Gal.3:14
That the blessing of Abraham might come upon the Gentiles in Christ Jesus, that we might receive the promise of the Spirit through faith.

John 4:13-14
Jesus answered and said to her, "Whoever drinks of this water will thirst again, but whoever drinks of the water that I shall give him will never thirst. But the water that I shall give him will become in him a fountain of water springing up into everlasting life."

Matt.3:11
I indeed baptize you with water unto repentance, but He who is coming after me is mightier than I, whose sandals I am not worthy to carry. He will baptize you with the Holy Spirit and fire.

Ezek.36:27
I will put My Spirit within you and cause you to walk in My statutes, and you will keep My judgments and do them.

Eph. 1:13
In Him you also trusted, after you heard the word of truth, the gospel of your salvation; in whom also, having believed, you were sealed with the Holy Spirit of promise.

Justice

Job 8:3
Doth God pervert judgment? or doth the Almighty pervert justice?

Job 37:23
Touching the Almighty, we cannot find him out: he is excellent in power, and in judgment, and in plenty of justice: he will not afflict.

Psalms 72:4
He shall judge the poor of the people, he shall save the children of the needy, and shall break in pieces the oppressor.

Psalms 89:14
Justice and judgment are the habitation of thy throne: mercy and truth shall go before thy face.

Isaiah 33:22
For the Lord is our judge, the Lord is our lawgiver, the Lord is our king; he will save us.

God's Promise Concerning...

Isaiah 56:1
Thus saith the Lord, Keep ye judgment, and do justice: for my salvation is near to come, and my righteousness to be revealed.

1 Corinthians 4:4
For I know nothing by myself; yet am I not hereby justified: but he that judgeth me is the Lord.

Knowledge

2 Chronicles 1:12
Wisdom and knowledge is granted unto thee; and I will give thee riches, and wealth, and honour, such as none of the kings have had that have been before thee, neither shall there any after thee have the like.

Job 36:4
For truly my words shall not be false: he that is perfect in knowledge is with thee.

Psalms 94:10
He that chastiseth the heathen, shall not he correct? he that teacheth man knowledge, shall not he know?

Proverbs 8:12
I wisdom dwell with prudence, and find out knowledge of witty inventions.

Proverbs 9:10
The fear of the Lord is the beginning of wisdom: and the knowledge of the holy is understanding.

Isaiah 33:6
And wisdom and knowledge shall be the stability of thy times, and strength of salvation: the fear of the Lord is his treasure.

Matthew 10:19
But when they deliver you up, take no thought how or what ye shall speak: for it shall be given you in that same hour what ye shall speak.

Colossians 1:10
That ye might walk worthy of the Lord unto all pleasing, being fruitful in every good work, and increasing in the knowledge of God;

Long life

Isaiah 46:4
*"Even to your old age and gray hairs I am he, I am he who will sustain you. I have made you and
I will carry you; I will sustain you and I will rescue you. "*

Proverbs 9:11
" For through me your days will be many, and years will be added to your life."

Psalm 91:16
With long life will I satisfy him, and show him my salvation.

Proverbs 3:1-2
My son, forget not my law; but let thine heart keep my

commandments: For length of days, and long life, and peace, shall they add to thee.

Psalms 21:4
He asked life of thee, and thou gavest it him, even length of days for ever and ever.

Deuteronomy 4:40
Thou shalt keep therefore his statutes, and his commandments, which I command thee this day, that it may go well with thee, and with thy children after thee, and that thou mayest prolong thy days upon the earth, which the Lord thy God giveth thee, for ever.

Deuteronomy 11:21
That your days may be multiplied, and the days of your children, in the land which the Lord sware unto your fathers to give them, as the days of heaven upon the earth.

Marriage

Genesis 2:18
And the Lord God said, "It is not good that man should be alone; I will make him a helper comparable to him."

Genesis 2:24
Therefore a man shall leave his father and mother and be joined to his wife, and they shall become one flesh.

Heb 13:4
Marriage honourable in all, and the bed undefiled.

Mark 10:7-9
'For this reason a man shall leave his father and mother and be joined to his wife, and the two shall become one flesh'; so then they are no longer two, but one flesh. Therefore what God has joined together, let not man separate.

Proverbs 18:22
Whoso findeth a wife findeth a good thing, and obtaineth favour of the Lord.

Proverbs 12:4
An excellent wife is the crown of her husband, but she who brings shame is like rottenness in his bones. Enjoy life with the wife whom you love, all the days of your vain life that he has given you under the sun, because that is your portion in life and in your toil at which you toil under the sun.

Song of Solomon 1:2
Let him kiss me with the kisses of his mouth for your love is more delightful than wine.

Isa 34:16
Search from the book of the Lord, and read: Not one of these shall fail; Not one shall lack her mate. For My mouth has commanded it, and His Spirit has gathered them.

God's Promise Concerning...

Psalms 128:3
Thy wife shall be as a fruitful vine by the sides of thine house: thy children like olive plants round about thy table.

Proverbs 31:11-12
The heart of her husband doth safely trust in her, so that he shall have no need of spoil. She will do him good and not evil all the days of her life.

1 Corinthians 7:14
For the unbelieving husband is sanctified by the wife, and the unbelieving wife is sanctified by the husband: else were your children unclean; but now are they holy.

Ephesians 5:25,28,31
Husbands, love your wives, even as Christ also loved the church, and gave himself for it; So ought men to love their wives as their own bodies. He that loveth his wife loveth himself. For this cause shall a man leave his father and mother, and shall be joined unto his wife, and they two shall be one flesh.

Peace

John 14:27
Peace I leave with you, my peace I give you. I do not give as the world gives. Do not let your hearts be troubled and do not be afraid."

Phil. 4:7
And the peace of God, which transcends all understanding, will guard your hearts and your minds in Christ Jesus.

Isaiah 26:3
Thou wilt keep him in perfect peace, whose mind is stayed on thee: because he trusteth in thee.

Romans 5:1
Therefore being justified by faith, we have peace with God through our Lord Jesus Christ:

Isaiah 26:12
Lord, thou wilt ordain peace for us: for thou also hast wrought all our works in us.

Isaiah 55:12
For ye shall go out with joy, and be led forth with peace: the mountains and the hills shall break forth before you into singing, and all the trees of the field shall clap their hands.

Psalms 37:37
Mark the perfect man, and behold the upright: for the end of that man is peace.

Romans 8:6
For to be carnally minded is death; but to be spiritually minded is life and peace.

Psalms 119:165
Great peace have they which love thy law: and nothing shall offend them.

Isaiah 57:2
He shall enter into peace: they shall rest in their beds, each one walking in his uprightness.

God's Promise Concerning...

Romans 14:17-19
For the kingdom of God is not meat and drink; but righteousness, and peace, and joy in the Holy Ghost. For he that in these things serveth Christ is acceptable to God, and approved of men. Let us therefore follow after the things which make for peace, and things wherewith one may edify another.

Psalms 37:11
But the meek shall inherit the earth; and shall delight themselves in the abundance of peace.

2 Corinthians 13:11
Finally, brethren, farewell. Be perfect, be of good comfort, be of one mind, live in peace; and the God of love and peace shall be with you.

Romans 15:13
Now the God of hope fill you with all joy and peace in believing, that ye may abound in hope, through the power of the Holy Ghost.

Isa.53:5
But He was pierced for our transgressions; He was crushed for our iniquities; the punishment that brought us peace was upon Him, and by His wounds we are healed.

Practical physical needs

Phil.4:19
And my God will meet all your needs according to His Glorious Riches in Christ Jesus.

Matt 6:25-27 NKJV
"Therefore I say to you, do not worry about your life, what you will eat or what you will drink; nor about your body, what you will put on. Is not life more than food and the body more than clothing? Look at the birds of the air, for they neither sow nor reap nor gather into barns; yet your heavenly Father feeds them. Are you not of more value than they? Which of you by worrying can add one cubit to his stature?

Matt.6:31-33
"Therefore do not worry, saying, 'What shall we eat?' or 'What shall we drink?' or 'What shall we wear?' For after all these things the Gentiles seek. For your heavenly Father knows that you need all these things. But seek first the kingdom of God and His righteousness, and all these things shall be added to you.

Deut.28:1,11,12
"Now it shall come to pass, if you diligently obey the voice of the Lord your God, to observe carefully all His commandments which I command you today, that the Lord your God will set you high above all nations of the earth. And the Lord will grant you plenty of goods, in the fruit of your body, in the increase of your livestock, and in the produce of your ground, in the land of which

the Lord swore to your fathers to give you. The Lord will open to you His good treasure, the heavens, to give the rain to your land in its season, and to bless all the work of your hand. You shall lend to many nations, but you shall not borrow.

Luke 12:30-31
For all these things the nations of the world seek after, and your Father knows that you need these things. 31 But seek the kingdom of God, and all these things shall be added to you.

Deut.29:9
Therefore keep the words of this covenant, and do them, that you may prosper in all that you do.

Ps 115:5
They have mouths, but they do not speak; Eyes they have, but they do not see.

Isa.1:19
If you are willing and obedient, You shall eat the good of the land.

Zech.10:1
Ask the Lord for rain In the time of the latter rain. The Lord will make flashing clouds; He will give them showers of rain, grass in the field for everyone.

Lev.26:3-5
'If you walk in My statutes and keep My commandments, and perform them, then I will give you

rain in its season, the land shall yield its produce, and the trees of the field shall yield their fruit. Your threshing shall last till the time of vintage, and the vintage shall last till the time of so wing; you shall eat your bread to the full, and dwell in your land safely.

Luke 12:24
Consider the ravens; They do not sow or reap, they have no store room or barn yet God feed them and how much more valuable you are than birds!

Phil 4:19
And my God shall supply all your need according to His riches in glory by Christ Jesus.

Luke 11:9
So I say to you, ask, and it will be given to you; seek, and you will find; knock, and it will be opened to you.

Ps.84:11-12
For the Lord God is a sun and shield; The Lord will give grace and glory; No good thing will He withhold From those who walk uprightly. O Lord of hosts, Blessed is the man who trusts in You.

Matt.6:32
For after all these things the Gentiles seek. For your heavenly Father knows that you need all these things.

Ps.37:3, 25
Trust in the Lord, and do good; Dwell in the land, and feed on His faithfulness. I have been young, and now am old; yet I have not seen the righteous forsaken, nor his descendants begging bread.

God's Promise Concerning...

Luke 12:30-31
For all these things the nations of the world seek after, and your Father knows that you need these things. But seek the kingdom of God, and all these things shall be added to you.

Luke 6:38
Give, and it will be given to you: good measure, pressed down, shaken together, and running over will be put into your bosom. For with the same measure that you use, it will be measured back to you.

Promotion

Deuteronomy 28:13
And the Lord shall make thee the head, and not the tail; and thou shalt be above only, and thou shalt not be beneath; if that thou hearken unto the commandments of the Lord thy God, which I command thee this day, to observe and to do them:

1 Samuel 2:8
He raiseth up the poor out of the dust, and lifteth up the beggar from the dunghill, to set them among princes, and to make them inherit the throne of glory: for the pillars of the earth are the Lord'S, and he hath set the world upon them.

Psalms 71:21
Thou shalt increase my greatness, and comfort me on every side.

Matthew 5:5
Blessed are the meek: for they shall inherit the earth.

Matthew 23:12
And whosoever shall exalt himself shall be abased; and he that shall humble himself shall be exalted.

Ephesians 2:6
And hath raised us up together, and made us sit together in heavenly places in Christ Jesus:

1 Peter 5:6
Humble yourselves therefore under the mighty hand of God, that he may exalt you in due time:

Prosperity

Deuteronomy 15:4
Except when there may be no poor among you; for the Lord will greatly bless you in the land which the Lord your God is giving you to possess as an inheritance.

Deuteronomy 15:6
For the Lord your God will bless you just as He promised you; you shall lend to many nations, but you shall not borrow; you shall reign over many nations, but they shall not reign over you

Deuteronomy 7:13
And He will love you and bless you and multiply you; He will also bless the fruit of your womb and the fruit of your land, your grain and your new wine and your oil, the increase of your cattle and the offspring of your flock, in the land of which He swore to your fathers to give you.

God's Promise Concerning...

Deuteronomy 28:3
Blessed shall you be in the city, and blessed shall you be in the country.

Deuteronomy 28:4
Blessed shall be the fruit of your body, the produce of your ground and the increase of your herds, the increase of your cattle and the offspring of your flocks.

Deuteronomy 28:5
"Blessed shall be your basket and your kneading bowl.

Deuteronomy 28:6
"Blessed shall you be when you come in, and blessed shall you be when you go out.

Deuteronomy 28:8
The Lord will command the blessing on you in your storehouses and in all to which you set your hand, and He will bless you in the land which the Lord your God is giving you.

Deuteronomy 28:11
And the Lord will grant you plenty of goods, in the fruit of your body, in the increase of your livestock, and in the produce of your ground, in the land of which the Lord swore to your fathers to give you.

Deuteronomy 28:12
The Lord will open to you His good treasure, the heavens, to give the rain to your land in its season, and to bless all the work of your hand. You shall lend to many nations, but you shall not borrow.

Deuteronomy 28:13
And the Lord will make you the head and not the tail; you shall be above only, and not be beneath, if you heed the commandments of the Lord your God, which I command you today, and are careful to observe them.

Deuteronomy 29:9
Therefore keep the words of this covenant, and do them, that you may prosper in all that you do.

Deuteronomy 30:5
Then the Lord your God will bring you to the land which your fathers possessed, and you shall possess it. He will prosper you and multiply you more than your fathers.

Deuteronomy 30:9
The Lord your God will make you abound in all the work of your hand, in the fruit of your body, in the increase of your livestock, and in the produce of your land for good. For the Lord will again rejoice over you for good as He rejoiced over your fathers,

Prov.3:5-6
Trust in the Lord with all your heart and lean not on your own understanding; in all your ways acknowledge Him and He will make your paths straight.

Jos.1:8; 2
This Book of the Law shall not depart from your mouth, but you shall meditate in it day and night, that you may observe to do according to all that is written in it. For then you will make your way prosperous, and then you will have good success.

God's Promise Concerning...

1 Kings 3:13
And I have also given you what you have not asked: both riches and honour, so that there shall not be anyone like you among the kings all your days.

1 Chronicles 29:12
Both riches and honour come from You, and You reign over all. In Your hand is power and might; in Your hand it is to make great and to give strength to all.

Nehemiah 9:21
Forty years You sustained them in the wilderness, so that they lacked nothing; their clothes did not wear out and their feet did not swell.

Nehemiah 9:25
And they took strong cities and a rich land, and possessed houses full of all goods, cisterns already dug, vineyards, olive groves, and fruit trees in abundance. So they ate and were filled and grew fat, and delighted themselves in Your great goodness.

Palm 1:3
He shall be like a tree Planted by the rivers of water, that brings forth its fruit in its season, whose leaf also shall not wither; And whatever he does shall prosper.

Psalm 5:12
For You, O Lord, will bless the righteous; with favour You will surround him as with a shield.

Psalm 23:1
The Lord is my shepherd; I shall not want.

Psalm 25:13
He himself shall dwell in prosperity, And his descendants shall inherit the earth.

Psalm 29:11
The Lord will give strength to His people; The Lord will bless His people with peace.

Psalm 34:9
Oh, fear the Lord, you His saints! There is no want to those who fear Him.

Psalm 34:10
The young lions lack and suffer hunger; But those who seek the Lord shall not lack any good thing.

Psalm 35:27
Let them shout for joy and be glad, who favour my righteous cause; And let them say continually, Let the Lord be magnified, Who has pleasure in the prosperity of His servant.

Psalm 37:25
I have been young, and now am old; yet I have not seen the righteous forsaken, Nor his descendants begging bread.

Psalm 50:10
For every beast of the forest is Mine, and the cattle on a thousand hills.

God's Promise Concerning...

Psalm 66:12
You have caused men to ride over our heads; we went through fire and through water; But You brought us out to rich fulfilment.

Psalm 67:7
God shall bless us, and all the ends of the earth shall fear Him.

Joel 2:26
You shall eat in plenty and be satisfied, and praise the name of the Lord your God, who has dealt wondrously with you; and my people shall never be put to shame.

Haggai 2:8
'The silver is mine, and the gold is Mine,' says the Lord of hosts.

Zachariah 8:12
For the seed shall be prosperous, the vine shall give its fruit, the ground shall give her increase, and the heavens shall give their dew. I will cause the remnant of this people to possess all these things.

Malachi 3:10
Bring all the tithes into the storehouse, that there may be food in My house, and prove Me now in this, says the Lord of hosts, If I will not open for you the windows of heaven And pour out for you such blessing That there will not be room enough to receive it.

Malachi 3:12
And all nations will call you blessed, for you will be a delightful land," says the Lord of hosts.

2 Peter 1:3
As His divine power has given to us all things that pertain to life and godliness, through the knowledge of Him who called us by glory and virtue,

3 John 1:2
Beloved, I pray that you may prosper in all things and be in health, just as your soul prospers.

Psalm 84:11
For the Lord God is a sun and shield; The Lord will give grace and glory; No good thing will He withhold From those who walk uprightly.

Psalm 68:6
God sets the solitary in families; He brings out those who are bound into prosperity; but the rebellious dwell in a dry land.

Psalm 68:19
Blessed be the Lord, Who daily loads us with benefits, The God of our salvation! Selah

Psalms 122:6-7
Pray for the peace of Jerusalem: they shall prosper that love thee. Peace be within thy walls, and prosperity within thy palaces.

Zechariah 1:17
Cry yet, saying, Thus saith the Lord of hosts; My cities through prosperity shall yet be spread a broad; and the Lord shall yet comfort Zion, and shall yet choose Jerusalem.

God's Promise Concerning...

Isaiah 48:17
Thus saith the Lord, thy Redeemer, the Holy One of Israel; I am the Lord thy God which teacheth thee to profit, which leadeth thee by the way that thou shouldest go.

Job 36:11
If they obey and serve Him, they shall spend their days in prosperity, and their years in pleasures.

2 Chronicles 26:5
He sought God in the days of Zechariah, who had understanding in the visions of God; and as long as he sought the Lord, God made him prosper.

2 Chronicles 31:21
And in every work that he began in the service of the house of God, in the law and in the commandment, to seek his God, he did it with all his heart. So he prospered.

2 Chronicles 1:12
Wisdom and knowledge are granted to you; and I will give you riches and wealth and honour, such as none of the kings have had who have been before you, nor shall any after you have the like."

Deuteronomy 8:9
A land in which you will eat bread without scarcity, in which you will lack nothing; a land whose stones are iron and out of whose hills you can dig copper.

2 Chron.20:20
So they rose early in the morning and went out into the Wilderness of Tekoa; and as they went out, Jehoshaphat stood and said, "Hear me, O Judah and you inhabitants

of Jerusalem: Believe in the Lord your God, and you shall be established; believe His prophets, and you shall prosper."

Eccl 5:19-20
As for every man to whom God has given riches and wealth, and given him power to eat of it, to receive his heritage and rejoice in his labor — this is the gift of God.

Gen 12:2
I will make you a great nation; I will bless you And make your name great; And you shall be a blessing.

Matt 6:33-34
But seek first the kingdom of God and His righteousness, and all these things shall be added to you. Therefore do not worry about tomorrow, for tomorrow will worry about its own things. Sufficient for the day is its own trouble.

Galatians 3:14
That the blessing of Abraham might come upon the Gentiles in Christ Jesus, that we might receive the promise of the Spirit through faith.

Genesis 9:7
And as for you, be fruitful and multiply; bring forth abundantly in the earth and multiply in it.

Eccl 3:13

God's Promise Concerning...

And also that every man should eat and drink and enjoy the good of all his labour — it is the gift of God.

Prov. 16:3
Commit your works to the Lord, And your thoughts will be established.

2 Cor 3:5,b
Not that we are sufficient of ourselves to think of anything as being from ourselves, but our sufficiency is from God.

1 Chron. 22:12-13
Only may the Lord give you wisdom and understanding, and give you charge concerning Israel, that you may keep the law of the Lord your God. Then you will prosper, if you take care to fulfil the statutes and judgments with which the Lord charged Moses concerning Israel. Be strong and of good courage; do not fear nor be dismayed.

Protection

Psalm 121:7, 8
"The Lord will keep you from all harm -- He will watch over your life; the Lord will watch over your coming and going both now and forevermore."

Isaiah 43:1,2
When you pass through the waters, I will be with you; and when you pass through the rivers, they will not sweep over you. When you walk through the fire, you will not be burned; the flames will not set you ablaze.

Psalms 4:8
I will both lay me down in peace, and sleep: for thou, Lord, only makest me dwell in safety.

Proverbs 1:33
But whoever listens to me will live in safety and be at ease, without fear of harm"

Psalms 41:2
The Lord will preserve him, and keep him alive; and he shall be blessed upon the earth: and thou wilt not deliver him unto the will of his enemies.

Psalms 91:3
Surely he shall deliver thee from the snare of the fowler, and from the noisome pestilence.

Psalms 91:14
Because he hath set his love upon me, therefore will I deliver him: I will set him on high, because he hath known my name.

Psalms 116:4
Then called I upon the name of the Lord; O Lord, I beseech thee, deliver my soul.

2Thess.3:3
But The Lord is Faithful and He will strengthen and protect you from the evil one.

2 Tim.4:18
*And the Lord will deliver me from every evil work and **preserve** me for His heavenly kingdom. To Him be glory forever and ever. Amen!*

Col.1:13
He has delivered us from the power of darkness and conveyed us into the kingdom of the Son of

His love

Col.2:15
Having disarmed principalities and powers, He made a public spectacle of them, triumphing over them in it.

1 John 5:18
We know that whoever is born of God does not sin; but he who has been born of God keeps himself, and the wicked one does not touch him.

Rom.8:38, 39
For I am persuaded that neither death nor life, nor angels nor principalities nor powers, nor things present nor things to come, nor height nor depth, nor any other created thing, shall be able to separate us from the love of God which is in Christ Jesus our Lord.

Ps.91:9-13
Because you have made the Lord, who is my refuge, Even the Most High, your dwelling place, No evil shall befall you, Nor shall any plague come near your dwelling; For He shall give His angels charge over you, To keep you in all your ways. In their hands they shall bear you up, Lest you dash your foot against a stone. You shall tread upon the lion and the cobra, The young lion and the serpent you shall trample underfoot.

Heb.2:14-15
Inasmuch then as the children have partaken of flesh and blood, He Himself likewise shared in the same, that through death He might destroy him who had the power of death, that is, the devil, and release those who through fear of death were all their lifetime subject to bondage.

Prov.18:10
The name of the Lord is a strong tower; the righteous run to it and are safe

1 Sam.2:9
He will guard the feet of His saints, But the wicked shall be silent in darkness. For by strength no man shall prevail.

Ps.125: 1-2
Those who trust in the Lord, Are like Mount Zion, Which cannot be moved, but abides forever. As the mountains surround Jerusalem, So the Lord surrounds His people From this time forth and forever.

Ps.91:3-4
Surely He shall deliver you from the snare of the fowler ,And from the perilous pestilence. He shall cover you with His feathers, And under His wings you shall take refuge; His truth shall be your shield and buckler.

Ps 91:11-12
For He shall give His angels charge over you, To keep you in all your ways. In their hands they shall bear you up, Lest you dash your foot against a stone.

God's Promise Concerning...

Ps.34:19-20
Many are the afflictions of the righteous, But the Lord delivers him out of them all. He guards all his bones; Not one of them is broken.

Ps.121:1-8
I will lift up my eyes to the hills From whence comes my help? My help comes from the Lord, Who made heaven and earth. He will not allow your foot to be moved; He who keeps you will not slumber. Behold, He who keeps Israel, Shall neither slumber nor sleep. The Lord is your keeper; The Lord is your shade at your right hand. The sun shall not strike you by day, Nor the moon by night. The Lord shall preserve you from all evil; He shall preserve your soul. The Lord shall preserve your going out and your coming in, From this time forth, and even forevermore.

Prov.29:25
The fear of man brings a snare, But whoever trusts in the Lord shall be safe.

Rest

Psalms 4:8
I will both lay me down in peace, and sleep: for thou, Lord, only makest me dwell in safety.

Psalms 23:2
He maketh me to lie down in green pastures: he leadeth me beside the still waters.

Proverbs 1:33
But whoso hearkeneth unto me shall dwell safely, and shall be quiet from fear of evil.

Proverbs 3:24
When thou liest down, thou shalt not be afraid: yea, thou shalt lie down, and thy sleep shall be sweet.

Isaiah 14:3
And it shall come to pass in the day that the Lord shall give thee rest from thy sorrow, and from thy fear, and from the hard bondage wherein thou wast made to serve,

Jeremiah 30:10
Therefore fear thou not, O my servant Jacob, saith the Lord; neither be dismayed, O Israel: for, lo, I will save thee from afar, and thy seed from the land of their captivity; and Jacob shall return, and shall be in rest, and be quiet, and none shall make him afraid.

Matthew 11:28-29
Come unto me, all ye that labour and are heavy laden, and I will give you rest. Take my yoke upon you, and learn of me; for I am meek and lowly in heart: and ye shall find rest unto your souls.

Restoration

Joel 2:25-26
And I will restore to you the years that the locust hath eaten, the cankerworm, and the caterpillar, and the palmerworm, my great army which I sent among you. And ye shall eat in plenty, and be satisfied, and praise the

name of the Lord your God, that hath dealt wondrously with you: and my people shall never be ashamed.

Job 42:10
And the Lord turned the captivity of Job, when he prayed for his friends: also the Lord gave Job twice as much as he had before.

Psalms 23:3
He restoreth my soul: he leadeth me in the paths of righteousness for his name's sake.

Psalms 40:2-3
He brought me up also out of an horrible pit, out of the miry clay, and set my feet upon a rock, and established my goings. And he hath put a new song in my mouth, even praise unto our God: many shall see it, and fear, and shall trust in the Lord.

Psalms 103:5
Who satisfieth thy mouth with good things; so that thy youth is renewed like the eagle's.

2 Corinthians 5:17
Therefore if any man be in Christ, he is a new creature: old things are passed away; behold, all things are become new.

Salvation

John 3:17
For God did not send His Son into the World to condemn it but to save the World through Him.

Rom 10:9-10
That if you confess with your mouth the Lord Jesus and believe in your heart that God has raised Him from the dead, you will be saved. For with the heart one believes unto righteousness, and with the mouth confession is made unto salvation.

Rom 10:13
For "whoever calls on the name of the Lord shall be saved."

Eph.2:8-9
For by grace you have been saved through faith, and that not of yourselves; it is the gift of God, not of works, lest anyone should boast.

1 Tim.2:3-4
For this is good and acceptable in the sight of God our Saviour, who desires all men to be saved and to come to the knowledge of the truth.

Heb.6:18
That by two immutable things, in which it is impossible for God to lie, we might have strong consolation, who have fled for refuge to lay hold of the hope set before us.

Titus 3:4-6 "
But when the kindness and love of God our Saviour appeared, he saved us, not because of righteous things we had done, but because of his mercy. He saved us through the washing of rebirth and renewal by the Holy Spirit, whom he poured out on us generously through Jesus Christ *our Saviour.*

2 Cor 5:17
Therefore, if anyone is in Christ, he is a new creation; the old has gone, the new has come.

Spiritual gifts

Rom.11:29
God's gifts and His call are irrevocable.

Rom 12:5-8
So we, being many, are one body in Christ, and individually members of one another. Having then gifts differing according to the grace that is given to us, let us use them: if prophecy, let us prophesy in proportion to our faith; or ministry, let us use it in our ministering; he who teaches, in teaching; he who exhorts, in exhortation; he who gives, with liberality; he who leads, with diligence; he who shows mercy, with cheerfulness.

Ephesians 4:8
Wherefore he saith, When he ascended up on high, he led captivity captive, and gave gifts unto men.

James 1:17
Every good gift and every perfect gift is from above, and cometh down from the Father of lights, with whom is no variableness, neither shadow of turning.

1 Corinthians 12:1
Now concerning spiritual gifts, brethren, I would not have you ignorant.

1 Corinthians 12:4
Now there are diversities of gifts, but the same Spirit.

1 Corinthians 12:28
And God hath set some in the church, first apostles, secondarily prophets, thirdly teachers, after that miracles, then gifts of healings, helps, governments, diversities of tongues.

1 Corinthians 14:12
Even so ye, forasmuch as ye are zealous of spiritual gifts, seek that ye may excel to the edifying of the church.

Exodus 31:3
And I have filled him with the spirit of God, in wisdom, and in understanding, and in knowledge, and in all manner of workmanship,

Success

Ecc 3:13
That everyone may eat and drink, and find satisfaction in all his toil--this is the gift of God."

Ecc 5:19
Moreover, when God gives any man wealth and possessions, and enables him to enjoy them, to accept his lot and be happy with his work- -- this is a gift of God."

Proverbs 8: 18,19
With me are riches and honour, enduring wealth and prosperity. My fruit is better than fine gold; what I yield surpasses choice silver."

God's Promise Concerning...

Joshua 1:8
This book of the law shall not depart out of thy mouth; but thou shalt meditate therein day and night, that thou mayest observe to do according to all that is written therein: for then thou shalt make thy way prosperous, and then thou shalt have good success.

Psalms 112:1-2
Praise ye the Lord. Blessed is the man that feareth the Lord, that delighteth greatly in his commandments. His seed shall be mighty upon earth: the generation of the upright shall be blessed.

Isaiah 58:11
And the Lord shall guide thee continually, and satisfy thy soul in drought, and make fat thy bones: and thou shalt be like a watered garden, and like a spring of water, whose waters fail not.

Widows

James 1:27
Pure religion and undefiled before God and the Father is this, To visit the fatherless and widows in their affliction, and to keep himself unspotted from the world.

Job 29:13
The blessing of him that was ready to perish came upon me: and I caused the widow's heart to sing for joy.

Deuteronomy 10:18
He doth execute the judgment of the fatherless and widow, and loveth the stranger, in giving him food and raiment.

Proverbs 15:25
The Lord will destroy the house of the proud: but he will establish the border of the widow.

Psalms 146:9
The Lord preserveth the strangers; he relieveth the fatherless and widow: but the way of the wicked he turneth upside down.

Jeremiah 49:11
Leave thy fatherless children, I will preserve them alive; and let thy widows trust in me.

Isaiah 54:5
For thy Maker is thine husband; the Lord of hosts is his name; and thy Redeemer the Holy One of Israel; The God of the whole earth shall he be called.

John 14:18
I will not leave you comfortless: I will come to you.

Psalms 68:5
A father of the fatherless, and a judge of the widows, is God in his holy habitation.

Deuteronomy 27:19
Cursed be he that perverteth the judgment of the stranger, fatherless, and widow. And all the people shall say, Amen.

John 16:22
And ye now therefore have sorrow: but I will see you again, and your heart shall rejoice, and your joy no man taketh from you.

God's Promise Concerning...

Mercy

Isaiah 30:18
...the Lord longs to be gracious to you; he rises to show you compassion. For the Lord is a God of justice. Blessed are all who wait for him!

Psalm 103:13
As a father has compassion on his children, so the Lord has compassion on those who fear him.

Lam 3:22-23
It is of the Lord's mercies that we are not consumed, because his compassions fail not. They are new every morning: great is thy faithfulness.

Matthew 6:14-15
For if you forgive men when they sin against you, your heavenly Father will also forgive you. But if you do not forgive men their sins, your Father will not forgive your sins.

1 John 1:9
If we confess our sins, he is faithful and just and will forgive us our sins and purify us from all unrighteousness."

Genesis 9:16
And the bow shall be in the cloud; and I will look upon it, that I may remember the everlasting covenant between God and every living creature of all flesh that is upon the earth.

Genesis 39:21
But the Lord was with Joseph, and shewed him mercy, and gave him favour in the sight of the keeper of the prison.

Exodus 33:19
And he said, I will make all my goodness pass before thee, and I will proclaim the name of the Lord before thee; and will be gracious to whom I will be gracious, and will shew mercy on whom I will shew mercy.

Deuteronomy 4:31
(For the Lord thy God is a merciful God;) he will not forsake thee, neither destroy thee, nor forget the covenant of thy fathers which he sware unto them.

Psalms 36:5
Thy mercy, O Lord, is in the heavens; and thy faithfulness reacheth unto the clouds.

Psalms 86:5-7
For thou, Lord, art good, and ready to forgive; and plenteous in mercy unto all them that call upon thee. Give ear, O Lord, unto my prayer; and attend to the voice of my supplications. In the day of my trouble I will call upon thee: for thou wilt answer me.

Psalms 145:8-9
The Lord is gracious, and full of compassion; slow to anger, and of great mercy. The Lord is good to all: and his tender mercies are over all his works.

God's Promise Concerning...

OTHER BOOKS BY ALLAN AND KATHY KIUNA

Anointed For The Market Place
by Bishop Allan Kiuna

Only 3% of Christians are called into full time service. The remaining 97% are called to the market place. It would be futile for God to create us and fail to empower us to fulfill His mission on earth. The first divine mandate for man was to be fruitful, multiply, replenish the earth and subdue it: and then have dominion. However, most of the territory that God wants the Christian believer to take over is currently occupied by some 'giants'. It is God's intention for the believers to venture into these territories, uproot the existing establishments, dethrone the secular giants and install God's order. This book is about how to leverage from God's available anointing to accomplish His end-time agenda in your place of calling.

Woman Without Limits
by Rev. Kathy Kiuna

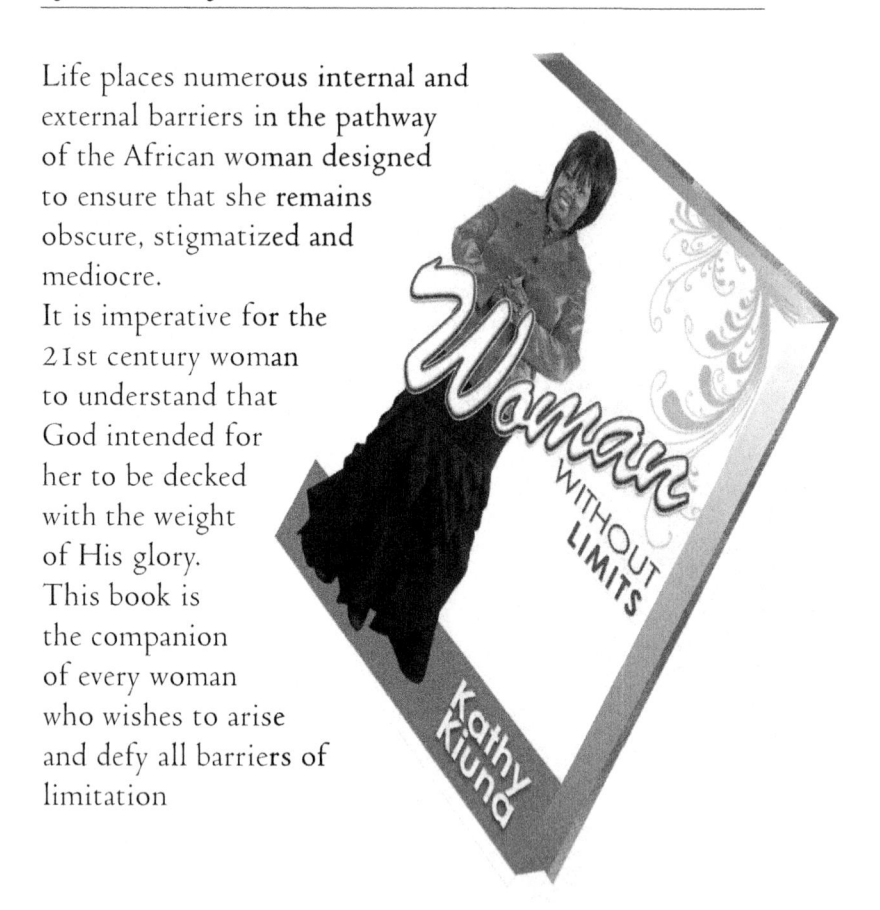

Life places numerous internal and external barriers in the pathway of the African woman designed to ensure that she remains obscure, stigmatized and mediocre.
It is imperative for the 21st century woman to understand that God intended for her to be decked with the weight of His glory. This book is the companion of every woman who wishes to arise and defy all barriers of limitation

Appointment With Destiny
Allani& Kathy Kiuna

As teenagers their lives were headed for certain disaster. Then two things happened; they met Jesus, and later each other. Their lives have never been the same since. *Appointment With Destiny* is the story of their individual struggles with alcohol and rebellion, and of their life changing encounter with God's saving grace. This is the story of severe trials that culminated in the birth of a great church. Allan and Kathy Kiuna are pastors and overseers of Jubilee Christian Church based in Nairobi Kenya. They are the proud parents of three children daughters: Vanessa, Stephanie; and son Jeremy

Celebrate Yourself
by Rev. Kathy Kiuna

blah blah blah blah blah blah blah blah blah
blah blah blah blah blah blah blah blah
blah blah blah blah blah blah blah
blah blah blah blah blah blah blah
blah blah blah blah blah blah
blah blah blah blah blah
blah blah blah blah blah
blah
blah blah blah blah blah
blah blah blah blah blah
blah blah blah blah blah blah
blah blah blah blah blah blah
blah blah

blah blah blah blah blah blah blah
blah blah blah blah blah blah blah
blah blah blah blah blah blah blah blah
blah blah
blah blah blah blah

blah blah blah blah blah blah blah blah blah
blah blah blah blah blah blah blah blah blah blah blah
blah blah blah blah blah blah blah blah blah blah blah
blah blah blah blah blah blah blah blah blah